We are now in the first century in the thirty-five million centuries of life on Earth in which one species can jeopardize the planet's future. In *Riders in the Storm: Ethics in an Age of Climate Change,* Brian Henning is right that the identity of the twenty-first century will increasingly be defined by long-festering ecological crises, made worse by political and market failures. Here is a basic introduction, full scale across science, politics, and economics, seeing climate change as both ethical failure and opportunity. His analysis is well researched and documented, well presented, and quite readable. *Riders in the Storm* joins the most forceful voices in this keystone concern on the global agenda.

—Holmes Rolston III
Colorado State University

In *Riders in the Storm: Ethics in an Age of Climate Change*, Brian Henning shows that we are called to rethink everything in view of the catastrophe we face so as to engage together in the great work to which Thomas Berry has been calling us. Central to honorable pursuit of this work is personal morality, and this morality must shape our lives to the needs of our times. Like every truly wise morality, what it calls for is not miserable sacrifice but joyful, responsible life. Much that he describes is familiar to long-time participants in the environmental movement.

—John Cobb Jr.
Claremont School of Theology

The century's task—a task set for us by that implacable master physics—is to make ourselves smaller. This book is an eloquent reflection on that beautiful chore.

—Bill McKibben, auth
Middlebury

RIDERS IN THE STORM

ETHICS IN AN AGE OF CLIMATE CHANGE

BRIAN G. HENNING

Author Acknowledgments

This project benefited greatly from the feedback and insights of the students in my Ethics of Global Climate Change at Gonzaga University from 2008 to 2014. The readability and flow of the initial manuscript was improved significantly thanks to the wise council of my wonderful development editor, Kathleen Walsh. The author extends his sincere thanks to the blind peer reviewers for their generous and exhaustive comments. Thanks go especially to all of the members of the production team at Anselm Academic for their professionalism, attention to detail, and hard work that made this volume a reality. Special thanks go to managing editor, Maura Hagarty, for her careful editor's eye and acquisitions editor, Jerry Ruff, for believing in the project from the start. Finally, I thank my wonderful spouse, Suzie Henning, without whose love, support, and encouragement this work would not be possible.

Some portions of this book originally appeared in journals or other books and are used with the permission of the publishers. Portions of chapter 1 and 4 were originally published as Brian G. Henning, "From Exception to Exemplification: Understanding the Debate over Darwin," in *Genesis, Evolution, and the Search for a Reasoned Faith*, edited by Mary Kate Birge et al. (Winona, MN: Anselm Academic, 2011). Portions of chapters 4 and 6 originally appeared as, Brian G. Henning, "Sustainability and Other Ecological Mistakes," in *Beyond Superlatives*, edited by Roland Faber, J. R. Hustwit, and Hollis Phelps, 76–89 (Newcastle upon Tyne: Cambridge Scholars Press, 2014). Portions of chapter 5 originally appeared as Brian G. Henning, "From Despot to Steward: The Greening of Catholic Social Teaching," in *The Heart of Catholic Social Teaching: Its Origins and Contemporary Significance*, edited by David Matzko McCarthy (Grand Rapids, MI: Brazos Press, 2009). The analysis in the appendix is an abbreviated version of Brian G. Henning, "Standing in Livestock's 'Long Shadow': The Ethics of Eating Meat on a Small Planet," *Ethics & the Environment* 16.2 (2011): 63–94.

Publisher Acknowledgments

Thank you to the following individuals who reviewed this work in progress:

Kendy Hess
College of the Holy Cross, Worcester, Massachusetts

Sarah Kenehan
Marywood University, Scranton, Pennsylvania

Created by the publishing team of Anselm Academic.

Cover images © *da-kuk/istockphoto.com* (stormy sea) and © *shayes17/istockphoto.com* (lighthouse)

Printed in the United States of America

7066

ISBN 978-1-59982-218-1

For Hope Philea and Nora Kalia.
May you take up the great work left to your generation.

Perhaps the most valuable heritage we can provide for future generations is some sense of the Great Work that is before them of moving the human project from its devastating exploitation to a benign presence. We need to give them some indication of how the next generation can fulfill this work in an effective manner. For the success or failure of any historical age is the extent to which those living at that time have fulfilled the special role that history has imposed upon them.

Thomas Berry, *The Great Work:*
Our Way into the Future

Contents

Abbreviations

ACUPCC	American College & University Presidents' Climate Commitment
CAFOs	concentrated animal feeding operations
cm	centimeter
CO$_2$	carbon dioxide
CO$_2$e	carbon dioxide equivalent
COP	Conference of the Parties
EPA	Environmental Protection Agency
FAO	Food and Agriculture Organization of the United Nations
ft	feet
GHG	greenhouse gases
IPCC	Intergovernmental Panel on Climate Change
m	meter
mpg	miles per gallon
NCAR	National Center for Atmospheric Research
NCDC	National Climatic Data Center
NOAA	National Oceanic and Atmospheric Administration
NSIDC	National Snow and Ice Data Center
OECD	Organisation for Economic Co-operation and Development
ppb	parts per billion
ppm	parts per million
RDA	recommended daily allowance
UNFCCC	United Nations Framework Convention on Climate Change
USDA	US Department of Agriculture
WCED	World Commission on Environment and Development

Preface

I first learned of global warming in the summer of 1992. As a rising high school junior from Boise, Idaho, I attended a policy debate preparation camp at Stanford University. The debate resolution under consideration for the 1992–93 school year was "Resolved: That the United States government should reduce worldwide pollution through its trade and/or aid policies."[1] Students from all over the country attended camps like the one at Stanford to collect evidence both for and against this resolution.

Although global warming came up as an area of research concerning worldwide pollution, it was just one among a long list of more traditional environmental issues such as air and water pollution, overpopulation, and deforestation.[2] Only four years earlier, in 1988, the United Nations Environment Programme and the World Meteorological Organization created the Intergovernmental Panel on Climate Change (IPCC) "to prepare a comprehensive review and recommendations with respect to the state of knowledge of the

---

1. "Past Policy Topics," National Speech and Debate Association, *http://bit.ly/1jYLsNm*.

2. This text uses the terms *global warming* and *global climate change* interchangeably. Scientists have migrated to the latter because it emphasizes that the increase in the global average surface temperature (global warming) does not manifest itself evenly across the globe (climate change). Since *climate change* itself sounds rather neutral (not all change is bad), some have suggested that *global climate disruption* might be an even more accurate phrase. For more on this, see "Frequently Asked Questions about Global Warming and Global Climate Change: Back to Basics," Environmental Protection Agency, *www.epa.gov/climatechange/Downloads/ghgemissions/Climate_Basics.pdf*. A 2014 study by the Yale Project on Climate Change Communication, "What's in a Name? Global Warming vs. Climate Change," found that "the term 'global warming' is associated with greater public understanding, emotional engagement, and support for personal and national action than the term 'climate change'" (*http://bit.ly/1wfarzH*).

science of climate change, social and economic impact of climate change, and possible response strategies and elements for inclusion in a possible future international convention on climate."[3] The IPCC issued its first assessment report on climate change in 1990, concluding that "there is a natural greenhouse effect which already keeps the Earth warmer than it would otherwise be" and that "emissions resulting from human activities are substantially increasing concentrations of the greenhouse gases carbon dioxide, methane, chlorofluorocarbons (CFCs) and nitrous oxide. These increases will enhance the greenhouse effect, resulting on average in an additional warming of the Earth's surface."[4]

As I sat down to write this book some twenty summers later, I realized that in many ways, human-induced climate change is not just one among many environmental challenges. Whereas the identity of much of the twentieth century was defined by two world wars, the twenty-first century will increasingly be defined by long-festering ecological crises. The specter of tyranny's march across Europe has been replaced by the inexorable rise of the oceans and the retreat of ice, as anthropogenic climate change threatens rising oceans, massive species extinction, and ecosystem collapse. These growing ecological crises will increasingly define this era. Human impact on the environment has now reached such a large magnitude that it threatens to disrupt much of the life on Earth.

After writing my first book, *The Ethics of Creativity: Beauty, Morality, and Nature in a Processive Cosmos*, which outlines a complex moral philosophy grounded in the work of Alfred North Whitehead (1861–1947), I set out to test its adequacy and applicability by considering how it might help people respond to a particular moral dilemma.[5] Having become interested in global warming, I decided I would research the topic more thoroughly. After five years of research, I realized that the threat of global climate change was too great to write a book aimed at a small audience of philosophers, as important as that work is. Having developed a course on the ethics

---

3. Intergovernmental Panel on Climate Change, "History," *http://bit.ly/1nxrB7L*.

4. Intergovernmental Panel on Climate Change, "Policymakers Summary," (1990), *http://bit.ly/1tLUE9C*.

5. Brian G. Henning, *The Ethics of Creativity: Beauty, Morality, and Nature in a Processive Cosmos* (Pittsburgh, PA: University of Pittsburgh Press, 2005).

of global climate change, I realized that although there were good texts by experts looking at the science, politics, economics, and ethics of global warming, there was no teaching text providing an introductory analysis of each of these areas in a single volume. From this realization came the idea for the present volume.[6]

Study of climate change is notoriously difficult. Complex and multifaceted, the challenge of global climate change is at once technological, scientific, economic, social, political, and moral. Indeed, to varying degrees, the study of global climate change involves nearly *every* branch of study. This presents a difficult challenge to scholars and the public alike. For scholars, there simply is no human who has sufficient expertise in all the relevant areas of study to write authoritatively about climate change. For the public, the scientific complexity and the spatial and temporal extendedness of climate change can make it difficult to comprehend. The problem of climate change is spatially and temporally extended in that it is a truly global problem (spatial) and it affects not only the present but many generations to come (temporal). Though the topic is global, to make the discussion more manageable and focused, I will largely, though not exclusively, draw on examples of responses to climate change from the United States (in chaps. 3–6).

Recognizing the fundamentally interdisciplinary nature of the challenge, this volume examines the basic scientific, political, economic, and moral dimensions of global climate change from an ethical perspective. Intended as an introduction to the topic, the initial chapters present in clear, accessible language the scientific understanding of climate change. Given this understanding, subsequent chapters consider the political, economic, and ethical responses to these scientific findings. In the end, this is a work of ethics.

As the philosopher Paul B. Thompson has noted, the term *ethics* is sometimes misunderstood in scientific contexts.[7] As a plural

---

6. Indeed, I penned the outline for this project while attending a conference on the theme "Brave New Planet: Imagining Ecological Communities" in Claremont, California. Between attending sessions by luminaries such as John Cobb, Bill McKibben, and David Orr, I called Anselm Academic editor, Jerry Ruff, and pitched the project. "Brave New Planet: Imagining Ecological Communities," Progressive Christians Uniting, October 28–29, 2011, *http://bit.ly/1tkc2Qw*.

7. Paul B. Thompson, "The Agricultural Ethics of Biofuels: The Food vs. Fuel Debate," *Agriculture* 2 (2012): 340, doi:10.3390/agriculture2040339.

noun the term refers to codes of conduct, often within a professional field. In this context, to act ethically often means little more than to act in accordance with a professional code of conduct. However, when philosophers use the term as a singular noun it refers to fundamental conceptions of how moral agents ought to act within their world relative to competing conceptions of what is good or has value. Thus, as Thompson notes, "While philosophical ethics does not necessarily shy away from prescriptive statements that say what people should be doing, the point of a philosophical analysis is to illustrate and analyze the background assumptions and context in which the prescription is grounded."[8] It is in this sense that the present analysis is ultimately a work of philosophical ethics.

I set out to write this book because I believe efforts to understand and respond to the challenge of global climate change will fall short unless and until humans begin the difficult work of reconceiving who they are and how they relate to the natural world. As the great cultural historian Thomas Berry (1914–2009) argued, bringing about this transformation is the "Great Work" of our age. What is needed are new ways of thinking and acting, grounded in new ways of understanding ourselves and our relationship to the world; ways of recognizing our fundamental interdependence and interconnection with everyone and everything in the cosmos, as well as the intrinsic beauty and value of every form of existence. We must not only pursue sustainability but also ask what it is that is worth sustaining? What does it mean to be a good steward on a planet that is 4.5 billion years old? Much hinges on whether our species can find meaningful answers to these questions; but first we must have the courage to confront them.

Brian G. Henning
June 2014
Gonzaga University
Spokane, Washington

---

8. Ibid.

CHAPTER

Climate Change Isn't Coming—It's Already Here

As I began to write this book in 2012 from the comfort of an air-conditioned neighborhood coffee shop in my little corner of the inland Northwest, much of the United States was baking in unprecedented temperatures.[1] Combined with lower-than-average precipitation, drought conditions covered 63% of the contiguous United States.[2] This mega-drought was so extensive that more than half (50.3%) of *all* US counties were declared disaster areas.[3] These hot, dry conditions and high winds also created the conditions for massive wildfires in many areas of the country. In July alone, more than 2 million acres (809,373 hectares) of forest burned nationwide. In Colorado, for instance, more than 34,500 people had to be evacuated from their homes, including entire towns; in the end, more than

1. Though the long-term trends are clear, climate change is difficult to describe because the data and literature are ever expanding. Readers are encouraged to consult the National Climatic Data Center to put current weather and climate patterns into historical context. See National Ocean and Atmospheric Administration, National Climatic Data Center, "State of the Climate," *www.ncdc.noaa.gov/sotc/*.

2. National Ocean and Atmospheric Administration, National Climatic Data Center, "State of the Climate: Global Analysis for July 2012," *www.ncdc.noaa.gov/sotc /global/2012/7*.

3. Michael Muskal, "As Drought Widens, 50.3% of U.S. Counties Declared Disaster Areas," *Los Angeles Times*, August 1, 2012, *http://lat.ms/1y0TbPL*.

350 homes were destroyed.[4] Although hot summers are nothing new, how does this one hot summer compare to the historical record?

It turns out that, for much of the country, July 2012 ranked among the warmest months on record. Figure 1.1 captures this temperature data. The closer the number on a state is to 118 (the number of years in the instrumental temperature record), the closer it is to being the hottest year on record for that state. According to the National Climatic Data Center (NCDC), the previous twelve months (August 2011 to July 2012) were the warmest since record-keeping began in 1895.[5] What is notable is not just the number of record-high temperatures, but just how high above normal they have been. For instance, the first six months of 2012 were 2.5°C (4.5°F) hotter than the average temperature and 0.83°C (1.5°F) hotter than the second hottest year on record (2006).[6]

This warming trend is not limited to the United States. The average land surface temperature in July 2012 for the Northern Hemisphere, where the majority of Earth's landmass is located, was the all-time warmest July on record. The Northern Hemisphere was 1.19°C (2.14° F) warmer than the twentieth-century average.[7] Thus putting the summer of 2012 in its historical context reveals that the increased temperature is not an isolated phenomenon. According to the NCDC, "July 2012 marks the thirty-sixth consecutive July and 329th consecutive month with a global temperature above the twentieth-century average."[8] Despite the day-to-day and season-to-season fluctuations, Earth *is* getting warmer. This is

4. Jennifer Oldham, Amanda J. Crawford, and Tim Jones, "Colorado Wildfire Forces 34,500 to Evacute as Homes Burn," *BloombergBusinessweek*, June 28, 2014, *http://buswk.co/1vhyFrR*.

5. National Oceanic and Atmospheric Administration, National Climatic Data Center, "State of the Climate: National Overview for June 2012," *www.ncdc.noaa.gov/sotc/national/2012/6*.

6. Kelly Slivka, "Record High Temperatures in First Six Months of the Year," *Green* (blog), *New York Times*, July 9, 2012, *http://nyti.ms/TQE7ox*.

7. "State of the Climate: National Overview for June 2012." The report also states, "The average global temperature across land and oceans during July 2012 was 0.62°C (1.12°F) above the 20th century average of 15.8°C (60.4°F) and ranked as the fourth warmest July since records began in 1880. The previous three months—April, May, and June—also ranked among the top five warmest for their respective months."

8. Ibid., 6.

July 2012 Statewide Ranks[9]

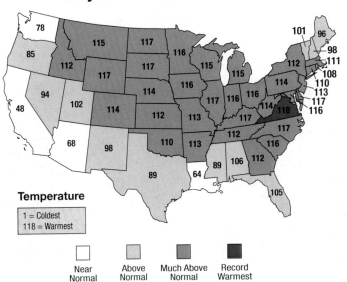

Temperature

| 1 = Coldest |
| 118 = Warmest |

Near Normal   Above Normal   Much Above Normal   Record Warmest

Figure 1.1. The closer the number on a state is to 118 (the number of years in the instrumental temperature record), the closer that state was to having the hottest year on record.

not disputable. Or, as the United Nations Intergovernmental Panel on Climate Change put it in their 2013 report, "Warming of the climate system is unequivocal."[10]

On Thin Ice

These persistently higher-than-normal global average surface temperatures are having detrimental effects on Earth's ecosystems. Nowhere is this more apparent than in the Arctic. Although the volume of ice has always fluctuated with the Arctic summer and winter, the ice cap at Earth's northern pole is steadily shrinking in

---

9. The data represented here is from the National Oceanic and Atmospheric Administration's National Climatic Data Center, *www.ncdc.noaa.gov.*

10. "Working Group I Contribution to the Fifth Assessment Report: Summary for Policymakers," *Climate Change 2013: The Physical Basis*, September 27, 2013, *www.climatechange2013.org/spm.*

size (see figs. 1.2 and 1.3). In fact, the summer of 2012 broke the previous record set in 2007 for the lowest volume of Arctic ice on record. This is no anomaly. Since satellite ice records began in 1979, the volume of ice has decreased steadily by 7.1% per decade. In other words, there is roughly 20% less sea ice now than thirty years ago.[11]

Figure 1.2. This satellite image shows the concentration of sea ice in September 1979 compared to the average sea ice minimum from 1979 through 2010 (depicted by orange line).

Figure 1.3. This satellite image shows the concentration of sea ice in April 2012 compared to the average sea ice minimum from 1979 through 2010 (depicted by orange line).

11. National Snow & Ice Data Center, "A Most Interesting Arctic Summer," 2012, *http://nsidc.org/arcticseaicenews/2012/08/a-most-interesting-arctic-summer/*.

Indeed, models created by researchers at the US Naval Postgraduate School estimate that there could be ice-free summers in the Arctic as early as 2016.[12]

While shipping, oil, and natural gas companies may benefit from the economic possibilities created by an ice-free or ice-diminished Arctic,[13] the people and creatures living in and around this area will not fare as well. For instance, without the sea ice to protect their coasts from the harsh winter waves, several Alaskan towns are at risk of falling into the ocean.[14] And animals such as walruses and polar bears, which hunt from ice floats, may become endangered or even extinct.

Reducing the **albedo** or whiteness of an area also raises concerns because a vicious warming cycle can be created (what scientists refer to as a **positive feedback** loop). Albedo relates to the reflectiveness of a surface. The higher the albedo, the greater the surface's reflectivity. Put simply, white surfaces reflect more of the incoming solar radiation into space than dark surfaces, such as green trees or open oceans, which absorb more of the Sun's rays. The warmer global temperatures shrink the surface area of the northern ice cap, revealing more open ocean, which has a lower albedo, which causes more of the Sun's rays to be absorbed, which increases warming, which further shrinks the amount of ice, continuing the cycle.

The Difference between Climate and Weather

Temperature records, both highs and lows, are broken every year. By its very nature, weather is variable. However, there is an important difference between **weather** and **climate**. Weather is the short-term, day-to-day variability within a particular geographical region that

---

12. David Schmalz, "NPS Researchers Predict Summer Arctic Ice Might Disappear by 2016, 84 Years ahead of Schedule," *Monterey County Weekly*, November 27, 2013, *http://bit.ly/1opVPvk.*

13. For example, the melting ice opens up new areas for oil exploration and drilling.

14. Shishmaref is one example of a coastal Alaskan village threatened by erosion because of a reduction in sea ice. See "Human and Economic Indicators—Shishmaref," *www.arctic.noaa.gov/detect/human-shishmaref.shtml.*

meteorologists using satellites can forecast up to ten days into the future, often with limited success. Climate, on the other hand, refers to long-term weather trends and patterns over continents or the entire planet. Climatologists, who study climate, emphasize atmospheric chemistry and reconstructed historical trends during decades, centuries, or even millenniums.[15]

Because of the immense complexity of Earth's systems, it is not possible to demonstrate that climate change causes a particular event, such as Hurricane Katrina (2005) or Hurricane Sandy (2012). However, changes in climate can influence the severity or frequency of such events. The correlation between smoking and cancer serves as a helpful analogy. Although research showed a statistical correlation between cigarette smoking and lung cancer as early as the 1950s, it took decades to scientifically prove that smoking causes cancer.[16] Even now, one cannot *prove* that Uncle Al's smoking habit caused his lung cancer. Doctors can only say that smoking greatly increases the *likelihood* of getting cancer and that Al's pack-a-day habit is *very likely* the reason for his lung cancer.[17] Similarly, strictly speaking, it is not possible to *prove* that global warming causes a given weather event such as a hurricane or drought, if by "prove" one means "demonstrate with absolute certainty." However, one can accurately say that pollution makes the atmospheric blanket "thicker" and traps more heat from the Sun at Earth's surface and that this increased global average temperature increases the *likelihood* of extreme weather events.

So, it is theoretically *possible* that the record high temperatures of the summer of 2012 result from **natural variability**. It is also *possible* that Uncle Al's pack-a-day smoking habit didn't cause his lung cancer but that it resulted from something else, perhaps an unknown

---

15. Some data, such as data on the Arctic ice, has been measured only since 1979. The National Center for Atmospheric Research has recorded data on temperatures across the globe only since 1960.

16. For a detailed and articulate analysis of the tobacco industry's misrepresentation of the scientific findings, see Naomi Oreskes and Erik M. Conway, *Merchants of Doubt: How a Handful of Scientists Obscured the Truth on Issues from Tobacco Smoke to Global Warming* (New York: Bloomsbury Press, 2010).

17. See sidebar "The Definition of Scientific Certainty" in chapter 2 for a discussion of scientific certainty.

genetic defect or an undetected environmental toxin. However, the likelihood that the higher incidence of lung cancer in chronic smokers is just a coincidence is exceedingly small. Likewise, the chance that the recent extreme weather events are due entirely to natural variability are exceedingly low—so low that it would be irresponsible to base decisions on them. Referring to the increasing incidence of extreme weather events, James Hansen, who for decades served as the top climate scientist in the United States, argues, "These weather events are not simply an example of what climate change could bring. . . . The odds that natural variability created these extremes are minuscule, vanishingly small. To count on those odds would be like quitting your job and playing the lottery every morning to pay the bills."[18]

Rolling the Climate Dice

When Hansen first testified about climate change to Congress in 1988, he introduced the idea of "climate dice" to help explain the difference between natural weather variability and the long-term trends of climate change.[19] "Natural variability" of the weather refers to the fact that some summers are really hot while others are mild, and some winters are very cold while others are warmer.[20]

To represent this natural variability, imagine that two of the six sides of a die represent colder-than-normal temperatures, two sides represent normal or average temperatures, and two sides represent warmer-than-average temperatures. Given these ratios, rolling the "climate dice" again and again should result in an even distribution of record-high temperatures and record-low temperatures. Some summers prove brutal while others are quite temperate. That is natural variability.[21]

18. James E. Hansen, "Climate Change Is Here–And Worse than We Thought," *Washington Post*, August 3, 2012, *http://wapo.st/1kHRrF6*.

19. Ibid.

20. Coincidently, while in 2012 nearly every state in the country experienced higher-than-normal temperatures, Washington was at or below the average of the last 118 years (see fig. 1.1).

21. Ibid.

However, as human pollution changes the composition of the atmosphere, extreme high temperatures become more and more likely, so much so that the die now has only one side with cooler-than-normal temperatures, one side with average temperatures, and *four* sides with warmer-than-normal temperatures. The climate dice are loaded. In fact, Hansen argues, the climate dice are now so loaded that one of those four warmer-than-normal sides represents not just hotter-than–normal temperatures but extremely hot temperatures: "Such events used to be exceedingly rare. Extremely hot temperatures covered about 0.1 percent to 0.2 percent of the globe in the base period of our study, from 1951 to 1980. In the last three decades, while the average temperature has slowly risen, the extremes have soared and now cover about 10 percent of the globe."[22]

This does not mean that there will no longer be severe, cold winters, or even record-setting ones. There will, but these events should not shift focus away from the overall trend, which clearly shows temperatures heading in an upward direction. The NCDC record shows the same trend. Statistically, in a climatically stable environment, the number of record-low temperatures should be about the same as the number of record-high temperatures over the course of a century. In the 1950s, record highs and lows, while not quite even, were fairly close (52 record highs with 48 record lows). However, when scientists at the National Center for Atmospheric Research (NCAR) examined millions of temperature readings from 1,800 weather stations across the United States over the six decades since 1950, they found that record highs outnumbered record lows, especially in the last thirty years. Between 2000 and 2009, scientists found twice as many record-high temperatures (291,237) as record-low temperatures (142,420).[23] This finding is notable not just for the

---

22. Ibid.

23. *AtmosNews*, National Center for Atmospheric Research, "Record High Temperatures Far Outpace Record Lows across U.S.," November 12, 2009, *http://bit.ly/1pfvP5Y*. "The study team analyzed several million daily high and low temperature readings taken over the span of six decades at about 1,800 weather stations across the country, thereby ensuring ample data for statistically significant results. The readings, collected at the National Oceanic and Atmospheric Administration's National Climatic Data Center, undergo a quality control process at the data center that looks for such potential problems as missing data as well as inconsistent readings caused by changes in thermometers, station locations, or other factors."

number of record-high temperatures but for the fact that there were more than twice as many days with record-high temperatures than record-cold temperatures. Therefore, according to the instrumental record of the last century, the climate of Earth is getting warmer, and at an accelerating rate.

How much has Earth's temperature increased over the last century? The increased incidence of extreme weather—such as the mega-drought of summer 2012 or "Superstorm" Sandy in November 2012—correlates with only a 0.8° C (1.44° F) increase in the average surface air temperature of Earth in the last century. On average, the twentieth century was almost 1°C (1.8°F) warmer than the nineteenth century. "Only one degree Celcius?" you might think to yourself. "Surely that isn't anything to be concerned about. After all, the temperature varies far more than that in a single day!"

I experienced daily temperature variation on a summer camping trip to Glacier National Park. Early morning temperatures in the forties (Fahrenheit) (4.4°C to 9.4°C) required multiple layers of clothes and warm hats. However, by late afternoon, the temperatures approached 90°F (32°C). If a fifty-degree (Fahrenheit) (28°C) change in temperature in one day is not out of the ordinary, why should anyone be concerned by a couple degrees' change in a century? Again, the key lies in appreciating the difference between weather and climate.

While *weather* can vary considerably, *climate* changes very slowly over long periods of time, often tens of thousands or hundreds of thousands of years. Large temperature fluctuations are common with weather, but even a small change in climate can cause great damage. So the more important question is, "Is a change of 0.8°C in the twentieth century a significant *climatic* change?" The answer is an unambiguous "Yes!" To understand why requires knowledge of the long-term climate cycles of Earth's geological past and a look back into Earth's "deep time."

Our Holocene Home

According to the best evidence available from physicists, the universe is approximately 13.75 billion years old. Earth itself did not even arrive on the cosmic scene until 4.5 billion years ago. Our species,

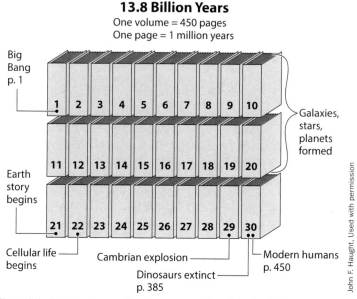

13.8 Billion Years
One volume = 450 pages
One page = 1 million years

Figure 1.4. These volumes of books represent time from the Big Bang to today. Notice the late appearance of humans.

Homo sapiens, is a relative latecomer, appearing only just 200,000 years ago. These vast stretches of cosmic time are difficult to comprehend. Georgetown University theologian John Haught provides an illustration helpful in representing this concept.

Imagine time represented as a series of books in which each page represents 1 million years and each volume has 450 pages. The total history of the universe would be represented by thirty volumes. The first twenty volumes of the history of the universe contain essentially lifeless physical and chemical processes that formed the first galaxies, stars, and terrestrial bodies. The story of Earth does not even begin until volume 21. Primitive, single-celled life forms arrived on the scene in volume 22. The so-called Cambrian explosion, a period of rapid speciation during which most major animal groups are believed to have developed, occurs at the end of volume 29 (550 million years ago), and the dinosaurs become extinct on page 385 of volume 30 (65 million years ago). *Homo sapiens* do not appear until two-thirds of the way down the *last page* of volume 30. Recorded human history begins at the start of the last line of text of the last page of volume 30.

Looking forward, the Sun is expected to have enough fuel to burn for another ten or eleven volumes (5 billion years) before it swells into a red giant, swallowing Earth and many other planets in the process.[24] It is important to recognize that, no matter what human beings do, Earth's story has both a beginning and an end, although humanity's role in that story is still being written.

Scientists who have attempted to reconstruct Earth's climatic history have noted a pattern of ice ages. Since an ice age is defined in part by the presence of large, land-based ice sheets, such as those in Greenland and Antarctica, Earth is technically still in the Quaternary ice age, which began approximately 2.58 million years ago. However, this ice age includes subcycles of approximately 40,000 to 100,000 years during which glaciers advance (glacial periods) and retreat (interglacial periods).[25] The current interglacial period, called the Holocene, began some 11,000 years ago. The Holocene is humanity's "normal." All recorded human history has taken place during this period. All the plants and animals on which humans depend are adapted to thrive in the temperate and relative climatic stability of the Holocene.[26]

Remarkably, the difference in the average global air temperature between the height of a glacial period and a warmer, interglacial period is only a change of 5°C to 6°C (9°F to 10.8°F).[27] In other words, if the average temperature of the planet were 6°C colder—as it was some 20,000 years ago during the last glacial maximum[28]—my home in Spokane, Washington, would likely be covered by hundreds

24. The previous two paragraphs originally appeared in Brian G. Henning, "From Exception to Exemplification: Understanding the Debate over Darwin," in *Genesis, Evolution, and the Search for a Reasoned Faith*, ed. Mary Kate Birge et al. (Winona, MN: Anselm Academic, 2011). See pages 92–94.

25. Chapter 2 will discuss what scientists believe might have caused these warming and cooling periods in the past and whether it is also the likely cause of the current warming.

26. Katherine Richardson et al., *Synthesis Report* from *Climate Change: Global Risks, Challenges & Decisions*, International Scientific Congress (March 10–12, 2009), 14, *http://bit.ly/1wwamru*.

27. John Houghton, *Global Warming: The Complete Briefing*, 4th ed. (Cambridge: Cambridge University Press, 2009), 13–14.

28. A "glacial maximum" is the "highest" point of a glacial period, after which ice starts to retreat.

Brian Henning, used with permission

Figure 1.5. Wild Goose Island, Saint Mary Lake, Glacier National Park.

of feet of ice. Indeed, during such a glacial period, pressure from massive ice floes carved the beautiful jagged peaks of Glacier National Park. These glaciers and ice sheets contained so much water that the oceans were some 400 feet (122 m) *lower* than they are today.[29] Some 125,000 years ago during the last warmer, interglacial period, Earth was even warmer than it is today and the oceans were some 13 to 19 feet (4 to 6 m) *higher* than they are today.[30] During these earlier glacial and interglacial periods, the contours of the present-day continents would have been unrecognizable. On this dynamic Earth, the only thing that remains constant is change.

Welcome to the Anthropocene

A better understanding of the climatic history of the planet can help answer the question raised earlier: "How do the current and projected

29. Houghton, *Global Warming*, 85.

30. Ibid.

changes in our climate compare to these historical changes?" The recent climate changes are extraordinary even in the context of such drastic changes in the past. The current change in climate is exceptional not merely for the increase in temperature—the temperature has been warmer in the past—but for the speed of change. The climate has gradually warmed since the end of the last glacial maximum some 20,000 years ago. According to climate scientist John Houghton, "The data indicate an average warming rate of about 0.2°C per century between 20,000 and 10,000 years before present (BP) over Greenland, with lower rates for other regions."[31] Therefore the 0.8°C (1.44°F) warming experienced in the twentieth century is at least four times the "background rate" of warming. Put differently, Earth experienced at least 400 years worth of warming in one century. Moreover, climate scientists project an *additional increase* in warming of 1.5°C to 6°C (2.7°F to 10.8°F) by the end of the twenty-first century.[32] That is, Earth will experience anywhere from one-third to an entire glacial period worth of temperature change—which normally takes many tens of thousands of years—in a single century.[33] Although a century represents a rather large increment of time for humans, this much temperature change in only one hundred years is truly extraordinary. Relating this to the shift in temperature experienced during my trip to Glacier National Park, it is as though the temperatures went from a chilly 40°F (4.4°C) to a toasty 90°F (32°C) in ten seconds, instead of ten hours.

Another, more personal analogy is to compare the difference in temperature fluctuation between weather and climate to the difference in temperature fluctuation between the body's surface (skin) temperature and the body's core temperature. In a sense, weather is to skin temperature as climate is to core body temperature.[34] In cold

---

31. Ibid., 88.

32. The Special Report on Emission Scenarios "shows increases for the different scenarios with best estimates for the year 2100 ranging from about 2°C to 4°C. When uncertainties are added, the overall likely range is from just over 1°C to 6°C—that wide range resulting from the large uncertainty regarding future emissions and also from uncertainty that remains regarding the feedbacks associated with the climate response to the changing atmospheric composition." Houghton, *Global Warming*, 143.

33. Ibid., 143–45.

34. The author thanks the students in his 2013 Ethics of Global Climate Change course at Gonzaga University for bringing this analogy to his attention.

weather, one's hands and feet can become quite chilled because as the body attempts to regulate a constant core temperature, the blood vessels in the extremities constrict, reducing blood flow. Thus the skin temperature of one's hands might be some 20°F to 30°F (9°C to 16°C) colder than one's core body temperature. On the other hand, core body temperature varies little, centering around 98.6°F (37°C). Thus large fluctuations in skin temperature are common, but even relatively small changes in core body temperature cause concern. For instance, if one were babysitting a young cousin and took her outside to play in the snow, her hands would be cold to the touch afterward. A thermal imaging camera might register their temperature at 60°F (15.5°C). A trip inside and a good mug of cocoa would quickly raise the skin temperature of her hands by 30°F (16.7°C). However, if that cousin starts to feel ill, one might take her core temperature. An increase of core body temperature (98.6°F or 37°C) of only a couple of degrees would cause worry; a change of 5°F (2.8°C) could prove life-threatening. The same holds true with climate.

Scientists predict that, were it not for the influence of humans, the climatic stability of the Holocene (that has made it possible for humans to thrive) would likely continue for several thousand years into the future.[35] However, the changes now underway are so large and so swift that some argue that the Holocene has prematurely ended and that Earth has entered a new climatic era. The Dutch atmospheric scientist Paul Crutzen has argued that, since **anthropogenic** (human-caused) changes now constitute the driving force behind changes on the planet, this new era should be called the "Anthropocene."[36] The author Bill McKibben argues that humanity no longer lives on the climatically stable and temperate planet called Earth but on a new, hotter, more dangerous planet, which he calls Eaarth.

> The planet on which our civilization evolved no longer exists. The stability that produced that civilization has vanished; epic changes have begun. . . . We *may*, with commitment and luck, yet be able to maintain a planet that will

---

35. Johan Rockström et al., "A Safe Operating Space for Humanity," *Nature* 461, no. 7263 (September 24, 2009): 472.

36. *Anthropos,* the ancient Greek term for "human," comes from the same root as found in "anthropology" and "misanthropic."

sustain *some kind* of civilization, but it won't be the same planet, and hence it can't be the same civilization. The earth that we knew—the only earth that we ever knew—is gone.[37]

Future Projections and Impacts

If the more intense heat waves, storms, and droughts *presently* experienced result from or are exacerbated by a 0.8°C (1.44°F) increase in Earth's average temperature, how much additional warming might occur this century, and how will it likely impact people and the planet?

At the beginning of the millennium, hundreds of scientists affiliated with the Intergovernmental Panel on Climate Change (IPCC) tried to answer this question. To aid world leaders responsible for making decisions for their countries, the IPCC created a "Special Report on Emission Scenarios." These forty scenarios are not predictions or forecasts but rather "projection scenarios" based on different possible courses of action this century. Extrapolating from correlations between past carbon dioxide (CO_2) levels, temperatures, and sea levels, scientists projected that, depending on the actions in the coming years, the average surface temperature would increase an additional 1.5°C to 6°C (2.7°F to 10.8°F) in the twenty-first century. Whether the final number ends up closer to one end of this range or the other depends largely on the policies adopted over the coming decades.

The average temperature of Earth has already increased by almost 1°C (1.8°F) during the last century, and at the current rate, will likely increase another 1.5°C to 6°C by the end of this century. That single degree has already brought about significantly warmer weather and increased the intensity of extreme weather events. If a single degree of warming has exacerbated the intensity of the droughts and storms, what will result from an increase of another 1°C to 6°C this century?

A planet with a changing climate will have regional winners and losers. While exile in Siberia will no longer be quite so bad, that Pacific island designated for an evil supervillain lair might disappear

37. Bill McKibben, *Eaarth: Making a Life on a Tough New Planet* (New York: Time Books, 2010), 27, emphasis in original.

underwater.[38] Although benefits and damages will be unevenly distributed, in general, far more people and ecosystems will emerge as "losers" than "winners." These unevenly distributed benefits and damages will also likely disproportionately affect poor people in developing nations. Indeed, those least responsible for climate change stand to suffer the most significant impact.

Climate is a complex, dynamic, living system, not a static machine, which makes it difficult to project the likely impacts of an increase in the average temperature of Earth. While some impacts may occur in a smooth, linear fashion, others may be non-linear, occurring more suddenly as certain "thresholds" or "safe operating boundaries" are crossed. Indeed, new evidence suggests that gradual changes to the climate might "prove to be the exception rather than the rule. Many subsystems of Earth react in a nonlinear, often abrupt, way, and are particularly sensitive around threshold levels of certain key variables."[39]

Examples of Effects of Global Average Temperature Change[40]

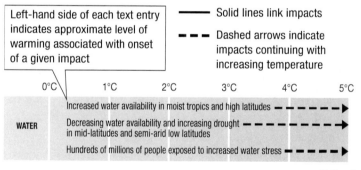

Continued

---

38. Low-lying island nations are already confronting this problem. Indeed, those living on the Carteret Islands have become the first "climate refugees" to lose their nation to rising seas. The documentary *Sun Come Up* is an excellent resource for understanding the plight of the Carteret Islanders. See "Additional Resources" at the end of this chapter.

39. Rockström et al., "Safe Operating Space," 472.

40. The data represented in this chart is from the Intergovernmental Panel on Climate Change, "Fourth Assessment Report: Summary for Policymakers," *Climate Change 2007: Synthesis Report*, http://bit.ly/SWzOXX.

Examples of Effects of Global Average Temperature Change *Continued*

	0°C	1°C	2°C	3°C	4°C	5°C

ECOSYSTEMS

Up to 30% of species at increasing risk of extinction ———— Over 40% — — ▶ of species become extinct

Increased coral bleaching ■— Most corals bleached ■— Widespread coral mortality — — — — ▶

Terrestrial biosphere tends toward a net carbon source as:
~15% ——————— ~40% of — — — ▶ ecosystem affected

Increasing species range shifts and wildfire risk

Changes to ecosystems due to weakening — — ▶ circulation in the north-south direction

FOODS

Complex, localized negative impacts on smallholders, — — — — — — — — ▶ subsistence farmers, and fishers

Productivity of some cereals ——————— Productivity of all — — ▶ decrease in low latitudes cereals decreases in low latitudes

Productivity of some cereals ■——— Cereal productivity increases at mid- to high latitudes decreases in some regions

COASTS

Increased damage from floods and storms — — — — — — — — — — — ▶

About 30% of global — — — ▶ coastal wetlands lost

Millions more people at risk of ■— — — — — — ▶ experiencing coastal flooding per year

HEALTH

Increasing burden from malnutrition, diarrhea, — — — — — — — — ▶ cardio-respiratory, and infectious diseases

Increased morbidity and mortality from heat waves, floods, and droughts — — — ▶

Changed distribution of some disease vectors ■— — — — — — — — — ▶

Substantial burden — — — — ▶ on health services

Figure 1.6. This chart presents examples of how different amounts of increased average global temperature changes—from 1 to 5 degrees Celsius—are expected to affect the world's climate in the twenty-first century. Scientists have a high level of confidence for all statements.

As indicated in figure 1.6, as the global average temperature increases, water availability will decrease and drought will increase in the mid-latitudes (the areas between roughly 25 and 65° North and 25 and 65° South, called the temperate zones) and semi-arid low latitudes (areas around the equator). As temperature increases, so does the rate of evaporation. Decreased water availability and increased evaporation will increase the risk and severity of wildfires. Increasing temperatures will also likely lead to increased human mortality from heat waves, floods, and droughts, as well as increasing malnutrition and diarrhea, cardio-respiratory, and infectious diseases. The combination of increased evaporation and decreased rainfall in some regions will also mean less water for agriculture and less run-off for waterways. In already semi-arid areas, this loss of rainfall will prove critical.[41] Beyond 2°C (3.6°F) warming, crops, which have adapted to the milder climate of the Holocene, will become less productive. For instance, rain-fed agriculture in Africa is expected to decrease 50% by 2020, exacerbating malnutrition.[42] Houghton notes that projected climate changes, combined with population increases, will double the number of people living in "severely stressed river basins . . . [from] 1.5 billion in 1995 to 3 to 5 billion" in 2050.[43]

Also, scientists expect the severity of storms to increase with each degree of warming: "For example, even with a modest increase in surface wind speed of 5 metres per second in tropical cyclones, possible with just a 1°C rise in ocean temperature, the number of the most intense and destructive cyclones [hurricanes] (Category 5) may double while the incidence of less intense cyclones would experience much smaller increases."[44] Although the regional effects will vary, many regions will experience less frequent but more severe precipitation events, resulting in damaging floods mixed with periods of intense drought, such as that experienced by more than half of the United States in 2012.[45]

Higher surface air temperatures, as well as higher concentrations of CO_2 in the atmosphere, also significantly impact Earth's oceans, which cover 70% of the planet. As the atmosphere becomes warmer, the oceans also become warmer. However, due to their size and the slow rate of turnover from the depths to the surface, the oceans respond more slowly than the atmosphere. These

---

41. Houghton, *Global Warming*, 190–91.

42. IPCC, "Fourth Assessment Report."

43. Houghton, *Global Warming*, 193.

44. Richardson et al., *Synthesis Report*.

45. Houghton states, "The likely result of such a drop in rainfall is not that the number of rainy days will remain the same, with less rain falling each time; it is more likely that there will be substantially fewer rainy days and considerably more chance of prolonged periods of no rainfall at all. Further, the higher temperatures will lead to increased evaporation reducing the amount of moisture available at the surface—thus adding to the drought conditions. The proportional increase in the likelihood of drought is much greater than the proportional decrease in average rainfall." *Global Warming*, 158–59.

warmer temperatures have many significant effects on climate and sea life. One of the most important impacts for humans is that warmer water takes up more room than cold water. Scientists refer to this as "thermal expansion." Even apart from the possible impact of melting land-based ice, this thermal expansion will cause the oceans to rise. According to one estimate, an increase of 2°C to 3°C (3.6°F to 5.4°F) by 2050 could cause 2.29 feet (70 cm) of sea level rise due to thermal expansion alone.[46] As a report by the non-profit, non-partisan organization Architecture 2030 notes, "Beginning with just one meter [3.2 ft.] of sea level rise, our nation would be physically under siege, with calamitous and destabilizing consequences. The U.S. is a coastal nation with over 12,000 miles of coastline. With 53 percent of all Americans living in and around coastal cities and towns, it is important to understand the impact of climate-induced sea level rise on our nation."[47] According to scientists, a large portion of the West Antarctic ice sheet has already "gone into irreversible retreat" and has passed "a point of no return."[48] Over the course of the next two centuries these melting glaciers could cause the oceans to rise 1.2 meters (4 ft).

Beyond 2°C to 3°C warming, some low-lying island nations are expected to disappear entirely, while low-lying nations such as Bangladesh will be inundated, creating tens of thousands of climate change refugees. Moreover, the impacts visited on future generations increase in severity the longer these high temperatures are maintained. For instance, temperature changes of 2°C to 5°C (3.6°F to 9°F) maintained for several thousand years could result in the

---

46. Oreskes and Conway, *Merchants of Doubt*, 178. Richardson and colleagues write, "An alternative approach is to base projections on the observed relationship between global average temperature rise and sea-level rise over the past 120 years, assuming that this observed relationship will continue into the future. New estimates based on this approach suggest a sea-level rise of around a metre [3.28 ft.] or more by 2100." *Synthesis Report*, 10. The IPCC reports, "Global average sea level has risen since 1961 at an average rate of 1.8 (1.2 to 2.3) mm/yr and since 1993 at 3.1 (2.4 to 3.8) mm/yr, with contributions from thermal expansion, melting glaciers and ice caps, and the polar ice sheets." "Fourth Assessment Report," 1.

47. *Architecture 2030*, "Hot Topics: Nation under Siege," *http://architecture2030.org /hot_topics/nation_under_siege*. This website includes an interactive map showing the affects of a one-meter rise in sea level on different American cities. Another interactive map can be found at *Surging Seas*, Climate Central, *http://sealevel.climatecentral.org/*.

48. Justin Gillis and Kenneth Chang, "Scientists Warn of Rising Oceans from Polar Melt," *New York Times*, May 12, 2014, *http://nyti.ms/1iGkKCF*.

complete elimination of the Greenland ice sheet, which would result in a sea level rise of about 7 meters (23 ft).[49] As later chapters will discuss, the multigenerational nature of this challenge makes it all the more difficult to address.

Quite apart from the effect of increasing ocean *temperature* is the role that increased concentration of atmospheric CO_2 has on the *chemistry* of the oceans; as the oceans absorb atmospheric CO_2, they become increasingly acidic.[50] (Think of the acidity of a carbonated drink.) **Acidification** threatens much ocean life. In particular, a lower pH (signifying higher acidity) seems to negatively impact the formation of coral polyps that form coral reefs. Ocean acidification combined with higher water temperature has resulted in coral reefs dying or "bleaching." The bleaching of the oceans' reefs is of concern not only because it results in the loss of beautiful and unique eco-systems but also because reefs are among the most biologically rich ecosystems, relied on by millions of people for both commercial and subsistence fishing. Beyond 3°C (5.4°F) warming, the IPCC predicts "widespread coral mortality" (see fig. 1.6).

As the oceans expand and glaciers retreat, the salty seawater will increasingly encroach on freshwater (a phenomenon called **salinization**), further exacerbating shortages. Storms will further erode coastlines, and encroaching water will displace more people. Beyond 3° warming, 30% of all coastal wetlands, among the most biologically diverse habitats on the planet, will disappear.

While some impacts become more severe with each degree increase, some changes are expected to be *irreversible*.[51] (Recall the

---

49. The IPCC reports, "The corresponding future temperatures in Greenland are comparable to those inferred for the last interglacial period about 125,000 years ago, when paleoclimatic information suggests reductions of polar and ice extent and 4 to 6 m of sea level rise." "Fourth Assessment Report," 13.

50. Houghton states, "The chemical laws governing this equilibrium are such that if the atmospheric concentration changes by 10% the concentration in solution in the water changes by only one-tenth of this: 1%." *Global Warming*, 40.

51. "Anthropogenic warming could lead to some impacts that are abrupt or irre-versible, depending upon the rate and magnitude of the climate change. Partial loss of ice sheets on polar land could imply metres of sea level rise, major changes in coastlines and inundation of low-lying areas, with greatest effects in river deltas and low-lying islands. Such changes are projected to occur over millennial time scales, but more rapid sea level rise on century time scales cannot be excluded." IPCC, "Fourth Assessment Report," 13.

analogy with the core temperature of the human body.) For instance, warming of 1°C to 3°C (1.8°F to 5.4°F) could lead to the extinction of 30% of all mammal, bird, and amphibian species in this century.[52] Warming beyond 4°C (7.2°F) would likely cause the extinction of more than 40% of all species on Earth. Species extinction is a natural part of the evolutionary process; biologists refer to this as the "background rate" of extinction. However, the current rate of species extinction is 50 to 500 times the typical background rate. Indeed, Earth may be in the midst of the sixth mass extinction event of its history:[53]

> There is growing understanding of the importance of functional biodiversity in preventing ecosystems from tipping into undesired states when they are disturbed. This means that apparent redundancy is required to maintain the ecosystem's resilience. Ecosystems that depend on a few or single species for critical functions are vulnerable to disturbances, such as disease, and are at a greater risk of tipping into undesired states.[54]

Given the magnitude and scope of the impacts of climate change, world leaders have agreed to try to limit warming to not more than an additional 2°C (3.6°F). They refer to this as the two-degree "guardrail,"[55] beyond which Earth would experience a "biodiversity catastrophe."[56]

---

52. "Climate change is *likely* to lead to some irreversible impacts. There is *medium confidence* that approximately 20–30 percent of species assessed so far are *likely* to be at increased risk of extinction if increases in global average warming exceed 1.5–2.5oC" (relative to 1980–99) (IPCC, "Fourth Assessment Report," 13).

53. Rockström et al., "Safe Operating Space," 473. See also Elizabeth Kolbert, *The Sixth Extinction: An Unnatural History* (New York: Henry Holt, 2014).

54. Rockström et al., "Safe Operating Space," 474.

55. Richardson and colleagues write, "While there is not yet a global consensus on what levels of climate change might be defined to be 'dangerous,' considerable support has developed for containing the rise in global temperature to a maximum of 2°C [3.6°F] above pre-industrial levels. This is often referred to as 'the 2°C guardrail.' . . . Beyond 2°C, the possibilities for adaptation of society and ecosystems rapidly decline with an increasing risk of social disruption through health impacts, water shortages and food insecurity." *Synthesis Report*, 12.

56. Richardson et al., *Synthesis Report*, 14. Chapter 2 will discuss what it would take to limit warming to only an additional 2°C this century. One estimate entails reducing global greenhouse gas emissions by 60–80% just to *limit* warming to 2–2.4°C (ibid., 18).

To better convey the uncertainty in climate change prediction and the role of policy decisions, researchers at MIT developed "Greenhouse Gamble" roulette wheels. These two wheels—one representing the status quo (policymakers make no changes addressing climate change) and one representing the implementation of strict climate change policies—"depict the estimated probability, or likelihood, of potential temperature change (global average surface temperature) over the next 100 years. The face of each wheel is divided into colored slices, with the size of each slice representing the estimated probability of the temperature change in the year 2100 falling within that range."[57] The category ("pie slice") on the "no policy" wheel representing less than a 3°C increase in temperature is the smallest slice on the wheel and is barely visible, and the two categories representing a temperature increase of 4°C–6°C cover nearly two-thirds of the wheel. In contrast, the categories (slices) on the "policy" wheel that represent less than a 3°C increase in temperature cover nearly nine-tenths of the wheel.[58] These wheels show that although there is uncertainty in predicting the future, we can change the set of probabilities we are operating under by implementing climate change policies.

The magnitude of the challenges global warming will likely cause in this century and for centuries to come raises questions about whether increases in temperatures will more likely be at the low end of 1°C to 2°C (1.8°F to 3.6°F) or the high end of 4°C to 6°C (7.2°F to 10.8°F). How big is the challenge humanity faces? In a sense, it depends on what humanity does or does not do over the next few decades. The next question to consider is: What is causing the global atmosphere to warm? Only by understanding the causes underlying these changes can humanity hope to mitigate them.

---

57. MIT Joint Program on the Science and Policy of Global Change Greenhouse Gamble Wheels, *http://globalchange.mit.edu/focus-areas/uncertainty/gamble*. On this interactive website you can "spin" the greenhouse gamble wheels to depict the estimated probability of potential temperature change over the next hundred years.

58. The "median value" of the "no policy" wheel is a 5.2°C (9.36°F) increase, while the median value of the "policy" wheel is an increase of 2.3°C (4.14°F). MIT Joint Program on the Science and Policy of Global Change Greenhouse Gamble Wheels. That is, without a climate change policy, there are only even odds (a 50/50 chance) of less than a 5.2°C temperature increase this century, which is at the very high end of the impact scenarios considered by the United Nations.

For Further Exploration

1. Visit one of these interactive maps and examine the expected flooding caused by rising sea levels:

   http://architecture2030.org/hot_topics/nation_under_siege

   > Architecture 2030 includes an interactive map showing the effects of a one-meter rise in sea level on different American cities.

   http://sealevel.climatecentral.org/

   > Surging Seas by Climate Central is an interactive map that allows users to look at effects of one to ten feet of sea level rise on coastal states.

   http://ngm.nationalgeographic.com/2013/09/rising-seas/ if-ice-melted-map

   > Rising Seas by National Geographic provides a view of the coastline of each continent should all the ice on the planet melt.

2. Review the latest US Global Change Research Program report (*http://ncadac.globalchange.gov/*) and identify the anticipated impacts of global climate change on your hometown.

3. Visit the MIT Joint Program on the Science and Policy of Global Change website (*http://globalchange.mit.edu/focus -areas/uncertainty/gamble*) and view the Greenhouse Gamble wheels. Then complete the following exercise, which the researchers described to Congress in 2007:

   > Imagine that you are playing "the greenhouse gamble" and have $100,000 in winnings. To end the game and collect your money, you must finally spin one of these two wheels. If you land on any of the sectors of the wheel corresponding to warming exceeding 3 degrees centigrade, you lose say $10,000 of your winnings. You can spin the "no policy" wheel for free but must pay to spin the "policy" wheel with its much lower odds of losing your money. In this game the $10,000 represents an (arbitrary) penalty for the damages caused by dangerous climate change and the money you are willing

to give up represents the cost of mitigating policy. How much of your $100,000 would you be willing to give up in order to spin the "policy" wheel?[59]

After deciding, spin the wheel and record your results and your reaction to your results.

Additional Resources

ORGANIZATIONS

350.org

This burgeoning global movement, co-founded by Bill McKibben and named for the amount of CO_2 scientists say will preserve a livable climate on Earth (350 parts per million), works to foster grassroots action to address climate change.

Intergovernmental Panel on Climate Change (IPCC)

The reports of this leading scientific body, which studies global climate change, are the most authoritative statements available. Its "Summary for Policymakers" documents are written in clear and accessible language that is understandable by non-scientists. See the following websites:

- IPCC website, *www.ipcc.ch/*
- IPCC's Fifth Assessment Report, *www.climate change2013.org/*
- An interactive time line of the IPCC and its work, *unfccc.int/timeline/*

National Climatic Data Center (NCDC)

This center maintains the world's largest climate data archive and provides climatological services and data to every sector of

---

59. Ronald G. Prinn, "Climate Change: A Growing Scientific Impetus for Policy," Testimony to the Committee on Ways and Means, US House of Representatives (February 28, 2007), *http://globalchange.mit.edu/files/document/MIT_R.Prinn.CT07.pdf*.

the US economy and to users worldwide. Readers are encouraged to consult the NCDC to put current weather and climate patterns into historical context. (See *www.ncdc.noaa.gov/.*)

National Center for Atmospheric Research (NCAR)

This center plans, organizes, and conducts atmospheric and related research programs in collaboration with universities. (See *http://ncar.ucar.edu/.*)

National Snow and Ice Data Center (NSIDC)

This center supports research on Earth's frozen realms: the snow, ice, glaciers, frozen ground, and climate interactions that make up Earth's cryosphere. (See *http://nsidc.org/.*)

BOOKS

Houghton, John. *Global Warming: The Complete Briefing.* 4th ed. Cambridge: Cambridge University Press, 2009.

This textbook, written by the founding co-chair of the IPCC, is one of the most helpful and accessible on the science of global climate change. It is especially well suited for non-scientists.

Kolbert, Elizabeth. *The Sixth Extinction: An Unnatural History.* New York: Henry Holt, 2014.

Kolbert argues that human activity is causing the sixth mass extinction event in Earth's history. The last such event was 65 million years ago when the dinosaurs went extinct.

McKibben, Bill. *Eaarth: Making a Life on a Tough New Planet.* New York: Time Books, 2010.

McKibben's use of the word "Eaarth" to refer to our planet highlights that through global warming Earth has become a new and different planet. He argues that fundamental change is the only hope for establishing balance on the planet.

———. *Oil and Honey: The Education of an Unlikely Activist.* New York: Times Books, 2013.

McKibben provides accounts of two strategies for fighting global climate change: participating in large-scale action and finding small-scale local solutions. He chronicles a fight against the fossil fuel industry as well as the work of beekeeping.

Oreskes, Naomi, and Erik M. Conway. *Merchants of Doubt: How a Handful of Scientists Obscured the Truth on Issues from Tobacco Smoke to Global Warming*. New York: Bloomsbury Press, 2010.

Oreskes and Conway construct a detailed and articulate analysis of the powerful negative effects when industry scientists create campaigns to systematically mislead the public on issues such as the health effects of smoking tobacco and the science of global climate change.

DOCUMENTARY

Sun Come Up

This Academy Award–nominated documentary follows the plight of the Carteret Islanders, who became the world's first climate change refugees when their island nation had to be abandoned due to rising seas. (See *www.suncomeup.com/.*)

2

CHAPTER

Understanding the Science of Climate Change

Earth's climate is a highly complex, interconnected system consisting of not only the thin layer of atmosphere surrounding the planet (if Earth were an onion, the atmosphere would only be as thick as the outer skin[1]) but also the land surface, oceans, and all living things.[2] As discussed in the previous chapter, Earth's climate has gone through many changes in its geological past. Ice ages and warmer inter-glacial periods are part of the natural variability of Earth's climate. This chapter seeks to determine what precipitated these changes in the past and whether these factors could also be causing the present changes. However, the controversy over global warming stems, in part, from confusion regarding the nature and purpose of scientific investi-gation and its conclusions. Thus, before examining the latest climate science, one must first look at what science is and how it works.

What Science Is (and Isn't)

Though it involves many forms of reasoning, at its root scientific investigation is an **inductive** form of investigation, meaning that it

---

1. Tim Flannery, *The Weather Makers: How Man Is Changing the Climate and What It Means for Life on Earth* (New York: Atlantic Monthly Press, 2005), 22.

2. Intergovernmental Panel on Climate Change, *Climate Change 2007: Synthesis Report*, 96, *http://bit.ly/1huLcQA*.

proceeds from particular observations to generalizations which are more or less probable based on the quality and quantity of those observations. For instance, scientists might have a hypothesis regarding the migratory habits of a given species of butterfly. They might explore this hypothesis by tracking the actual migratory path of a sample of the butterflies, perhaps by creating a clever way of tagging some of them. The results would be carefully collected, recorded, and analyzed. If all of the tagged butterflies take the same basic migratory route, scientists might draw the conclusion (generalization) that the other, unobserved butterflies of that species also took the same migratory route. The analysis of these **facts** would then either confirm or disconfirm the initial hypothesis. These facts are taken as **evidence** that either confirms or disconfirms the hypothesis.

In their collaboration, *Merchants of Doubt*, Naomi Oreskes, professor of history and science studies at the University of California, San Diego, and Erik Conway, a historian at NASA's Jet Propulsion Laboratory at the California Institute of Technology, liken this process of scientific inquiry to a court case.

> A scientific hypothesis is like a prosecutor's indictment; it's just the beginning of a long process. The jury must decide not on the elegance of the indictment, but on the volume, strength, and coherence of the evidence to support it. We rightly demand that a prosecutor provide evidence—abundant, good, solid, consistent evidence—and that the evidence stands up to the scrutiny of a jury of peers, who can take as much time as they need.[3]

Science, they go on to note, works in a similar way. A scientific hypothesis is only considered established when a qualified jury of peers consider all of the evidence and deem it sufficient. This **peer review** process is the cornerstone of scientific research. In their evaluation, experts in the field (peer reviewers) consider many factors, such as whether there are mistakes in the way data were gathered or interpreted, whether the study demonstrates awareness

---

3. Naomi Oreskes and Erik M. Conway, *Merchants of Doubt: How a Handful of Scientists Obscured the Truth on Issues from Tobacco Smoke to Global Warming* (New York: Bloomsbury Press, 2010), 32.

of other relevant research, whether it follows proper methodology, and whether the data collected are sufficient to support the conclusion drawn from them. Only after the intense scrutiny of the blind peer-review process can a scientific claim be considered legitimate.

However, the act of publishing the results does not establish the absolute truth of a scientific hypothesis. Scientists publish the results of their findings to share them with other scientists in the field, who then try to repeat the results. That is, other scientists try to see if they can falsify the results. For example, in observing the same species of butterfly, do others also find that it takes the same migratory route? If after decades of careful investigation by multiple scientists, no observation fails to confirm a given hypothesis—if every butterfly of a given species is observed to fly a given migratory route—the hypothesis might be elevated to the level of a **scientific theory**. If a scientific hypothesis is tested and retested over decades and even centuries, then it might be elevated to the level of a **scientific law**.

This scientific meaning of the term *theory* differs greatly from its popular meaning. Saying, "I have a theory about who will win the NCAA men's basketball tournament," is quite different than a scientist talking about the "theory of gravity." A scientific theory is a hypothesis that, after decades of careful research, has never failed to be confirmed by observation. Or to put it in the positive form, every observation during a long period of time has been consistent with the theory. Thus a scientific theory is not a guess but an extremely likely claim based on decades of carefully documented and analyzed evidence. A scientific theory is nearly the opposite of a guess or "theory" about who will win the big game.

However, referring to a scientific claim as a theory or even a law does not change the fact that a scientific hypothesis is ultimately an inductive claim supported by a body of particular observations over a given time. Calling a scientific hypothesis a scientific theory or a scientific law does not establish absolute certainty. There is a vast divide between "very certain" and "absolutely certain." As an inductive form of investigation that moves from particular observations to generalizations, science does not and cannot deal in the currency of absolutes. Its claims are statistical probabilities. This is no slight on science but simply the nature of inductive investigation. It cannot arrive at absolutely certain claims. Every scientific claim is either more or less certain, depending on the strength of the evidence (particular facts/observations) that confirm it.

Given this understanding of science, strictly speaking, it is not accurate to say that a scientific *theory* is proven or a fact. Philosophers refer to such claims as **category errors**. Individual observations (facts) that confirm a hypothesis serve as proof in support of a theory, but theories are never proven in the sense of being absolutely certain. Facts are particular observations that may or may not support a theory, but theories themselves are not facts. So particular observations are individual facts that either confirm or disconfirm a given hypothesis. If the *facts* confirm the hypothesis, they are taken as *evidence* or proof in support of the hypothesis. If after many years, a hypothesis fails to be disconfirmed, then it might be considered a well-established *theory* or eventually a *law*. However, again strictly speaking, theories are not facts, and they are not proven.

That science cannot achieve absolute certainty does not impeach its worth. On the contrary, this open-ended, recursive, self-correcting feature of science is exactly what makes it one of the most powerful means to understand the world. If multiple scientists continually observe evidence that contradicts a given hypothesis, then ultimately the hypothesis/theory/law must change, not the facts. Even the most widely accepted natural laws are not immune to revision. For centuries scientists took Newton's laws of motion as absolutely certain, until Albert Einstein showed that they are only partially correct. And the advent of quantum mechanics has further demonstrated that Einstein's relativity theories are themselves only partially adequate. The importance of scientific claims is only weakened when they are considered to have a degree of certainty that they cannot achieve.

The theories of evolution, gravity, and anthropogenic climate change are neither proven nor a fact. They are extremely likely generalizations supported by vast numbers of facts that thousands of different scientists have carefully documented, analyzed, and tested during a period of many decades. The facts provide proof in support of the theories but do not themselves prove the theories. To say otherwise represents a misuse of the terms *fact* and *proof.*

The work of the Intergovernmental Panel on Climate Change (IPCC) reflects this understanding when it concludes, "Warming of the climate system is unequivocal, and since the 1950s, many of the observed changes are unprecedented over decades to millennia. The atmosphere and ocean have warmed, the amounts of snow and ice have diminished, sea level has risen, and the concentrations of greenhouse gases have increased."[4] The planet *is* getting warmer. This is a fact, or to be more precise, the "facts" (particular observations) reveal that the planet is indeed getting warmer (see chap. 1). This leads to the question, what is causing this warming? What hypothesis best explains the facts? According to the IPCC, "Human influence has been detected in warming of the atmosphere and the ocean, in changes in the global water cycle, in reductions in snow and ice, in global mean sea level rise, and in changes in some climate extremes. . . . It is *extremely likely* that human influence has been the dominant cause of the observed warming since the mid-20th century."[5] The shift in language is significant. The report refers to the initial claim that Earth is warming as "unequivocal" but notes that it is "extremely likely" that this warming is caused by anthropogenic greenhouse gas emissions. The former is categorical (all-or-nothing) and the latter is statistical (more-or-less). (See sidebar "The Definition of Scientific Certainty" on page 48.)

Consensus vs. Consilience

When many different researchers support a scientific claim, policymakers and reporters commonly refer to the **consensus** among scientists. For instance, one might note the consensus among biologists that natural selection is a primary cause of speciation (evolution) or the consensus among astrophysicists that the universe exploded into existence from a singularity some 13.8 billion years ago (the Big Bang). In the case of climate research collected and reported by the IPCC, the term *consensus* proves particularly apt. In addition to synthesizing top researchers' individual studies performed throughout the world, the IPCC deliberately includes in its working groups political representatives from member nations. To make its findings helpful to policymakers and presumably to decrease debate and disagreement

---

4. Intergovernmental Panel on Climate Change, *Climate Change 2013: The Physical Science Basis*, *www.climatechange2013.org/*.

5. Ibid., emphasis in original.

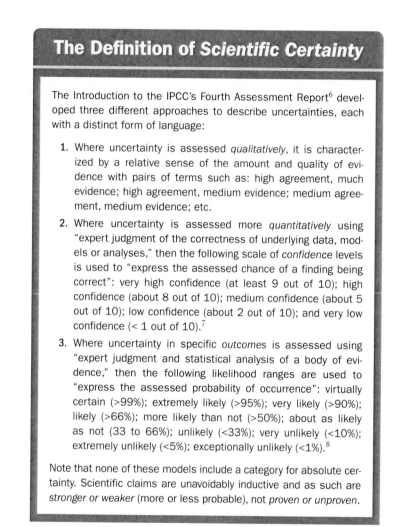

The Definition of *Scientific Certainty*

The Introduction to the IPCC's Fourth Assessment Report[6] developed three different approaches to describe uncertainties, each with a distinct form of language:

1. Where uncertainty is assessed *qualitatively*, it is characterized by a relative sense of the amount and quality of evidence with pairs of terms such as: high agreement, much evidence; high agreement, medium evidence; medium agreement, medium evidence; etc.

2. Where uncertainty is assessed more *quantitatively* using "expert judgment of the correctness of underlying data, models or analyses," then the following scale of *confidence* levels is used to "express the assessed chance of a finding being correct": very high confidence (at least 9 out of 10); high confidence (about 8 out of 10); medium confidence (about 5 out of 10); low confidence (about 2 out of 10); and very low confidence (< 1 out of 10).[7]

3. Where uncertainty in specific *outcomes* is assessed using "expert judgment and statistical analysis of a body of evidence," then the following likelihood ranges are used to "express the assessed probability of occurrence": virtually certain (>99%); extremely likely (>95%); very likely (>90%); likely (>66%); more likely than not (>50%); about as likely as not (33 to 66%); unlikely (<33%); very unlikely (<10%); extremely unlikely (<5%); exceptionally unlikely (<1%).[8]

Note that none of these models include a category for absolute certainty. Scientific claims are unavoidably inductive and as such are *stronger or weaker* (more or less probable), not *proven or unproven*.

about its findings, the IPCC requires unanimity among both scientists and political representatives when crafting their "Summary for Policymakers" of the scientific research. The IPCC will not publish a

6. IPCC, *Climate Change 2007*.

7. Ibid.

8. Ibid.

report without agreement (consensus) among the participants, so its five complete assessment reports certainly do represent a consensus among nations and scientists regarding the state of the climate.[9]

Consensus, however, involves compromise and agreement in the political or social spheres. This concept is utterly alien to basic scientific investigation. As scientist James Lovelock warns, "Do not suppose that conventional wisdom among scientists is similar to consensus among politicians and lawyers. Science is about the truth and should be wholly indifferent to fairness or political expediency."[10] Indeed, Lovelock is not alone in arguing that the political consensus model adopted by the IPCC has resulted in assessment reports that dramatically *understate* the problem of climate change. Critics point out that if the summaries of the work of the IPCC require the approval of political delegates from countries economically dependent on oil revenue, such as Saudi Arabia or Qatar, it seems very likely that any achievable consensus will be watered down.[11]

Although the IPCC's desire to have political consensus regarding the results of scientific research seems a laudable goal, many scientists agree that in the end, science has no room for political agreement or posturing. Either the facts support a given conclusion

---

9. John Houghton states, "No previous scientific assessments on this or any other subject have involved so many scientists so widely distributed both as regards their countries and their scientific disciplines. The IPCC Reports can therefore be considered as authoritative statements of the contemporary views of the international scientific community." He continues, "A further important strength of the IPCC is that, because it is an intergovernmental body, governments are involved in its work. In particular, government representatives assist in making sure that the presentation of the science is both clear and relevant from the point of view of the policymaker. Having been part of the process, governments as well as scientists are in a real sense owners of the resulting assessments—an important factor when it comes to policy negotiations." *Global Warming: The Complete Briefing*, 4th ed. (Cambridge: Cambridge University Press, 2009), 265.

10. James Lovelock, *The Vanishing Face of Gaia: A Final Warning* (New York: Basic Books, 2009), 11.

11. Only the Summary for Policymakers (SPM) goes through this approval process. The synthesis of the scientific evidence itself does not go through a similar process. Nevertheless, since the summaries characterize the overall importance and meaning of the evidence, this is a potentially significant problem. See, for instance, IPCC, *Climate Change 2013*, which presents the 33-page SPM, as well as the full report, which is 1,535 pages. For an interesting inside account of this process, see John Broome, "A Philosopher at the IPCC," International Society for Environmental Ethics (website), May 20, 2014, *http://bit.ly/RxDr59*.

or they do not. While scientists can and should explain their findings in the inherently political marketplace of ideas, ultimately science works best when it explains clearly what the current research indicates and resists the urge to overstate or oversimplify its findings. In the end, what scientists *believe* does not really matter; what their *research* finds is what matters. That is, the *consensus* of climate scientists is less important than the *consilience* of their evidence.

Consilience refers literally to the "jumping together" of many independent lines of investigation. Oreskes likens consilience to the multiple forms of evidence in a court case (e.g., DNA evidence, fingerprints, eyewitness reports, videos) that all support a single conclusion. Considered in isolation, no single line of evidence would be sufficient to convict a person or establish his or her guilt or innocence beyond a reasonable doubt. So too, all evidence taken together does not prove any conclusion with absolute certainty. However, a consilience of the evidence around a single conclusion does provide a strong reason for confidence in that conclusion. If DNA evidence, fingerprints, eyewitnesses, and videos all confirm Colonel Mustard committed the murder in the library with the candlestick, then there is good reason for detaining and trying him for the crime. Being based on a consilience of evidence, scientific arguments are more like a cable than a chain. Whereas a chain is only as strong as its weakest link, the many twisted strands of a cable can support immense weight, even if some of the strands fail. If research from, among other things, ice cores, lakebed sediment, tree rings, ocean water temperature and chemistry, air temperature, coral polyps, and satellites all independently suggest that the atmosphere is warming at an accelerating rate and that anthropogenic emissions are the main cause, then the consilience of evidence makes that conclusion extremely likely.

Thus, on closer examination, the IPCC's reports are more careful than the popular discussion of climate change might suggest. The IPCC does not speak in terms of absolutes. Rather, IPCC scientists use qualitative language in their reports to indicate the degree of certainty or the degree of likelihood of their conclusions. This scale has no 100% and no 0%. (See sidebar "The Definition of *Scientific Certainty*" on page 48.) Science never reaches absolute certainty or absolute proof. Scientific claims ultimately represent probabilities of greater or lesser magnitude, which raises cautions about waiting to act until a given phenomenon (e.g., global warming) has been "proven." As Oreskes and Conway assert: "Science is never finished, so the relevant policy question is always whether the available evidence is *persuasive*, and whether the established facts outweigh the residual uncertainties. This is a judgment call."[12] Given this background, then, are the facts in support of the theory of anthropogenic climate change persuasive?

The Basics of Climate Science

Over long periods of time dramatic variability in Earth's climate is quite natural. Given this, one might wonder, "Could the warming that Earth is currently experiencing just be natural?" Answering this question requires an understanding of the causes behind past ice ages and interglacial periods.

Global Warming: Who Turned Up the Heat?

Scientists have identified three primary candidates to explain the rise in the surface temperature of Earth: changes in solar output (also known as total solar irradiance), changes in Earth's orbit, and changes in the composition of Earth's atmosphere. Any one of these (or combinations of them) could explain the present increase.

Changes in solar output. The Sun, which goes through cyclical changes that scientists are only beginning to understand, would seem the most likely culprit for climate changes. While changes in the Sun's output could certainly cause global warming, "the output of the sun itself has *not* changed to any large extent over the last million years or so."[13] Indeed, if anything, the Sun has been in a period of relatively low activity for decades. Based only on the Sun, Earth should probably be cooling slightly, not warming.

Changes in Earth's orbit. Even if the total solar irradiance has not increased appreciably, changes in Earth's orbit could affect Earth's climate. Indeed, it seems likely that many of the ice ages in Earth's past were probably not caused by changes in the quantity of solar

---

12. Oreskes and Conway, *Merchants of Doubt*, 76.

13. Houghton, *Global Warming*, 85, emphasis added.

radiation but in the distribution of that radiation, due to three different types of cycles of Earth's orbit. These three orbital variations, referred to as **Milankovitch cycles** for the Serbian mathematician who posited them, are (a) the "eccentricity" of Earth's orbit or the "flatness" of its elliptical orbit, which has a 100,000-year period; (b) the tilt of its axis (obliquity) from 21.6° to 24.5°, which has a 42,000-year period; and (c) the perihelion (axial precession) or the season during which Earth is facing the Sun, which has a 23,000-year period.[14] (See fig. 2.1.) Though other factors also play a role,

Milankovitch Cycles[15]

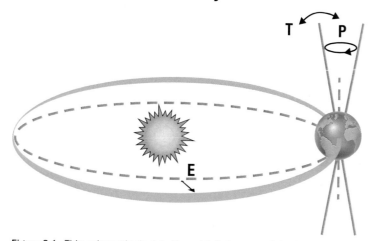

Figure 2.1. This schematic depicts the orbital changes of the Earth that have the most effect on ice age cycles. "E" denotes the eccentricity or shape of orbit. "T" denotes the axial tilt of the Earth. "P" denotes precession or the orientation of Earth relative to the Sun.

---

14. Houghton writes, "As the Earth's orbit changes its relationship to the Sun, although the total quantity of solar radiation reaching the Earth varies very little, the distribution of that radiation with latitude and season over the Earth's surface changes considerably. . . . Careful study of the correlation between the two curves [between summer sunshine and ice volume] demonstrates that 60 percent of the variance in the climatic record of global ice volume falls close to the three frequencies of regular variations in the Earth's orbit, thus providing support for the Milankovitch theory." *Global Warming*, 85–86.

15. The information for this image is from IPCC, "Frequently Asked Questions," *www.ipcc.ch/publications_and_data/ar4/wg1/en/faq-6-1.html.*

these natural variations in Earth's orbit—not, for instance, changes in the concentration of greenhouse gases—explain why Earth has gone into or come out of periods of glaciation approximately every 100,000 years.

Might these orbital variations explain the present warming? Yes. Milankovitch cycles certainly could cause global warming, but they are not the cause of the present warming. Indeed, considering only its orbital cycles, Earth should have had a "longer than normal interglacial period leading to the beginning of a new ice age perhaps in 50,000 years' time."[16] In other words, despite significant natural variation in Earth's climate, the rapid warming in the twentieth and twenty-first centuries cannot be explained either by changes in the Sun's radiation output or in Earth's orbit.

Changes in the composition of Earth's atmosphere. Since the present warming trend does not result from changes in solar output or from changes in Earth's orbit, the most likely culprit seems to be changes in the composition of the atmosphere. The chapter will now discuss in detail changes observed in Earth's atmosphere including the greenhouse house effect—how it occurs naturally and how it has been enhanced.

The Greenhouse Effect, Natural and Enhanced

The Sun emits ultraviolet or shortwave radiation. Roughly one-third of incoming solar radiation never reaches the surface of Earth but is reflected into space by Earth's atmosphere. The remaining two-thirds of incoming solar radiation is absorbed by Earth's surface and to a lesser extent by the atmosphere itself.[17] The lighter the surface's color, the more likely it will reflect the incoming radiation back into space. This refers to the albedo or literally the "whiteness" of a surface. Anyone who has noticed the difference between wearing a black shirt and a white shirt on a sunny summer day has experienced the albedo effect.

Surfaces release absorbed incoming solar radiation as infrared or "longwave" radiation. Some infrared radiation that organisms, land, ice, and oceans emit is released into space, but much of it is absorbed by gas molecules in the atmosphere and radiated back to

---

16. Houghton, *Global Warming*, 87.

17. IPCC, *Climate Change 2007*, 115.

Earth.[18] Scientists refer to this as the **greenhouse effect** because the molecules in the atmosphere function in much the same way as the panes of glass do in a greenhouse. The glass lets in shortwave solar radiation but traps the longwave radiation, making the temperature inside the greenhouse much warmer than the air outside (see fig. 2.2). Parking a car in the sun with the windows up offers a quick way to see this greenhouse effect in action.

The science behind the greenhouse effect has been studied for more than 150 years and is well understood by scientists.[19]

© daulon/Shutterstock.com

Figure 2.2. This diagram illustrates aspects of the atmospheric greenhouse effect. The yellow lines indicate shortwave or ultraviolet radiation. The red lines indicate longwave or infrared radiation. The curved blue lines in the sky represent the atmosphere, which traps longwave radiation.

18. Ibid.

19. Oreskes and Conway write, "In the mid-nineteenth century, Irish experimentalist John Tyndall first established that CO_2 is a greenhouse gas—meaning that it traps heat and keeps it from escaping to outer space. He understood this as a fact about our planet, with no particular social or political implications. This changed in the early twentieth century, when Swedish geochemist Svante Arrhenius realized that CO_2 released to the atmosphere by burning fossil fuels could alter the Earth's climate, and British engineer Guy Callendar compiled the first empirical evidence that the 'greenhouse effect' might be detectable. In the 1960s, American scientists started to warn our political leaders that this could be a real problem, and at least some of them—including Lyndon Johnson—heard the message. Yet they failed to act on it." *Merchants of Doubt*, 170.

The greenhouse effect is not only a naturally occurring phenomenon but also one that is vital to life on Earth. Without it, Earth's average surface temperature would be around -6°C (21.2°F), instead of the current and much more pleasant 15°C (59°F).[20] Without the greenhouse effect, Earth would be frozen to its equator—not a pleasant place for warm-blooded mammals to live.

This greenhouse effect is not unique to Earth but can also be observed on Mars and Venus. As scientists have discovered from robotic rovers such as NASA's *Curiosity* (see chap. 4, fig. 4.3), it is likely that Mars has water, but in the absence of any significant atmosphere, that water can't exist in liquid form. What appear to be gullies cut by running water suggests that this may not have always been the case. Venus, on the other hand, has the opposite problem: "Within the Venus atmosphere, which consists very largely of carbon dioxide, deep clouds consisting of droplets of almost pure sulphuric acid completely cover the planet and prevent most of the sunlight from reaching the surface."[21] Venus's atmosphere is so thick it traps any sunlight that reaches its surface, making its surface temperature more than 500°C (932°F).[22] Venus offers an example of what scientists call the "runaway greenhouse effect."

Without the natural greenhouse effect, therefore, most organisms alive today would find Earth uninhabitable. Since humanity's Industrial Revolution and the discovery of internal combustion engines, humans have released large quantities of gases into the atmosphere, amplifying the naturally occurring greenhouse effect. In a sense, the atmosphere works like a blanket on a bed during the winter. The air on top of the blanket is cold, but a person underneath the blanket is much warmer because the blanket traps body heat. The temperature gets increasingly warmer with each additional blanket because less body heat can escape. The atmosphere works in a similar way. The increasing concentration of heat-trapping gases—so-called greenhouse gases (GHG)—in the atmosphere makes the atmosphere "thicker," similar to adding another blanket to the pile, so less longwave radiation can be emitted into space.

---

20. Houghton, *Global Warming*, 20.

21. Ibid., 27.

22. Ibid.

Earth's atmosphere consists mostly of nitrogen (approximately 75%) and oxygen (approximately 20%).[23] However, the gases most responsible for the greenhouse effect—carbon dioxide (CO_2), methane (CH_4), and nitrous oxide (N_2O)[24]—make up a very small percentage of the overall atmosphere. In fact, scientists do not measure them in terms of percentages but in terms of parts per million (ppm) or, in the case of nitrous oxide, parts per billion. Therefore if one were to count one million molecules of gas in the atmosphere, more than 400 of them would be CO_2, 1.9 would be methane, and so on.[25]

TABLE 2.1

Atmospheric Concentration of Greenhouse Gases[26]

Gas	Preindustrial levels (pre-1750)	2012–13
	ppm=parts per million, ppb=parts per billion	
Carbon dioxide (CO_2)	280 ppm	395 ppm
Methane (CH_4)	722 ppb	1893 ppb
Nitrous oxide (N_2O)	270 ppb	326 ppb
Chlorofluorocarbons (CFCs)	0	236 ppb
Ozone (O_3)	237 ppb	337 ppb

23. Ibid., 21. According to Houghton, as of 2007, 78% of the atmosphere was nitrogen (N_2) and 21% oxygen (O_2).

24. There are other anthropogenic sources of greenhouse gases, such as chlorofluorocarbons (CFCs).

25. For current atmospheric concentrations of all greenhouse gases, consult the Carbon Dioxide Information Analysis Center, "Recent Greenhouse Gas Concentrations," *http://cdiac.ornl.gov/pns/current_ghg.html*.

26. Ibid. The CO_2 value is the average for 2013. The concentrations of the other gases are averages for 2012.

Of these three gases (CO_2, methane, and nitrous oxide), CO_2 is the most important. It has contributed approximately 72% of the enhanced or anthropogenic greenhouse effect to date, with methane being responsible for 21% and nitrous oxide about 7%.[27] For at least the last 650,000 years, the concentration of CO_2 in the atmosphere has been within 20 ppm of about 280 ppm.[28] However, since the Industrial Revolution, humans have disrupted the balance of CO_2, releasing more than 600,000 million tons (600 gigatons) through the burning of fossil fuels.[29] This has increased the concentration of carbon in the atmosphere by more than one-third, from around 280 ppm in 1700 to more than 400 ppm in 2014.[30]

One could visualize this by thinking of the atmosphere as a gigantic bathtub into which waste gases are poured. The tub's drain represents the processes that remove these waste gases from the atmosphere. As noted in chapter 1, some of these greenhouse gases are destroyed in the atmosphere. Others, namely CO_2, are absorbed by the oceans or removed from the atmosphere by organisms such as trees and plants. The rate at which the atmospheric "tub" is filling depends on whether the rate of waste gases going in exceeds the rate of nature's ability to remove them. At present, the level of gases (the concentration of greenhouse gases) is rapidly rising. For instance, the concentration of CO_2 in the atmospheric bathtub has historically been about 280 ppm, while a level of 350 ppm would still make it possible to achieve relative climatic stability (see fig. 2.3). Furthermore, scientists believe that the concentration of CO_2 would need to stay below 400 ppm to keep warming below 2°C (3.6°F) this century. Having already exceeded 400 ppm in 2014, atmospheric CO_2 is higher than it has been for at least 650,000 years.[31] The natural ability of Earth to absorb waste gases has been exceeded, and the "water" is pouring over the sides of the atmospheric "tub."

27. Houghton, *Global Warming*, 35.

28. Ibid., 37.

29. Ibid.

30. To check the current concentration of atmospheric CO_2, visit *http://co2now.org/*.

31. Houghton, *Global Warming*, 37.

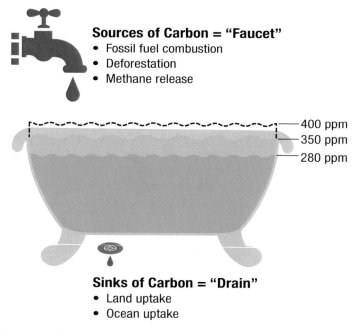

Carbon Bathtub

Sources of Carbon = "Faucet"
- Fossil fuel combustion
- Deforestation
- Methane release

400 ppm
350 ppm
280 ppm

Sinks of Carbon = "Drain"
- Land uptake
- Ocean uptake

Figure 2.3. The atmosphere can be likened to a large tub. The level of the "water" rises if CO_2 is added faster than nature can "drain" it. The top of the tub represents the greatest concentration of CO_2 compatible with climatic stability, which is estimated at 350 ppm.

The quantity of carbon released into the atmosphere, however, represents only one variable. The other variable concerns how long it stays in the atmosphere once released; scientists call this the "carbon cycle." Unlike other gases, which are broken down in the atmosphere, CO_2 is merely redistributed.[32] Carbon stays in the atmosphere until removed by some process. Depending on the process, this can take anywhere from days (for carbon "taken up" by land plants) to millennia (for carbon "taken up" by the deep ocean). This gives carbon a relatively long life cycle in the atmosphere—100 years

---

32. On the time scales under discussion here, anthropogenic carbon emitted into the atmosphere as CO_2 is not destroyed but redistributed among the various carbon reservoirs. CO_2 is therefore different from other greenhouse gases that are destroyed by chemical action in the atmosphere. See ibid.

on average.[33] Thus much of the carbon currently warming the planet was released by earlier generations, and much of the carbon released today will still be warming the planet more than a century from now.[34]

Whereas CO_2 concentrations in the atmosphere have increased by more than one-third over preindustrial levels, the concentration of methane has more than doubled in the last two centuries.[35] Methane forms through anaerobic breakdown of organic matter, a process not dependent on oxygen and fueled by bacteria found in environments such as flooded soils, wetlands, digestive tracts, termite mounds, and landfills. Thus methane comes from both "natural" sources—most importantly, wetlands and termite mounds—as well as anthropogenic sources, including coal mines, leakage from natural gas pipelines and wells, oil wells, rice paddies, intentional biomass burning (burning of organic matter such as wood or peat, often to create pasture or feed crops), as well as the treatment of manure and enteric fermentation (flatulence from ruminant animals such as cows, goats, and sheep raised for food).[36] Though still present in the atmosphere in far smaller amounts than CO_2 (1.775 ppm vs. 400 ppm), methane plays a disproportionate role in global warming, contributing 21% of all anthropogenic warming.[37] The reason stems from differences in the molecular properties of atmospheric methane.

Unlike CO_2, which is gradually "taken up" by land plants or the ocean, methane is chemically broken down in the atmosphere, lasting an average of only twelve years.[38] This relatively short life cycle is

---

33. Houghton writes that the time can "range from less than a year to decades (for exchange with the top layers of the ocean and the land biosphere) to millennia (for exchange with the deep ocean or long-lived soil pools)." Ibid., 37.

34. As will be discussed in later chapters, this temporal dimension of the greenhouse effect creates unique ethical challenges because what humans do today will affect people and ecosystems for generations.

35. Houghton, *Global Warming*, 20 and 50.

36. Ibid., 50. For a breakdown of methane emission by source, see ibid., 53, table 32.

37. Ibid., 35.

38. As the Fourth Assessment Report of the IPCC explains, "Most CH_4 is removed from the atmosphere by reaction with the hydroxyl free radical (OH), which is produced photochemically in the atmosphere." IPCC, *Fourth Assessment Report*, Working Group I (2007), *http://bit.ly/1wppjKS*. Given the rate of this chemical process, the average lifetime of a molecule of atmospheric methane is twelve years, which is much shorter than that of carbon dioxide and other greenhouse gases such as nitrous oxide (N_2O), which has a 114-year lifetime. Ibid., *http://bit.ly/1kouYi1*.

offset by the fact that methane proves far more potent at trapping heat than CO_2. Indeed, molecule-for-molecule, methane traps twenty-five times as much heat as CO_2. Given the different life cycles and potencies of these greenhouse gases, scientists have found it useful to develop the notion of the "global warming potential" (GWP) of various gases (see table 2.2). By comparing the lifetime and potency of various gases to CO_2, scientists have created a single metric, which they call CO_2 equivalent (CO_2e), for measuring greenhouse gas emissions.

TABLE 2.2

Greenhouse gas global warming potentials (GWPs) relative to CO_2 for a time horizon of 100 years[39]

Greenhouse Gas	Lifetime (years)	GWP
Carbon Dioxide (CO_2)	Variable[40]	1
Methane (CH_4)	12	25
Nitrous Oxide (N_2O)	114	298

Therefore, what can be said about global warming? First, it is a fact that the planet is getting warmer and that this is causing climate change. Second, although changes in solar output or Earth's orbit (Milankovitch cycles) could cause this warming, there is no evidence that they actually do. Third, no one who understands the science doubts the existence of the naturally occurring greenhouse effect, which keeps Earth more than 20°C warmer (36°F) than it would be otherwise. Fourth, human activities have released large

---

39. Ibid., 212, *www.ipcc.ch/publications_and_data/publications_ipcc_fourth_assessment_report_synthesis_report.htm.*

40. As the IPCC explains, "Carbon dioxide (CO_2) is exchanged between the atmosphere, the ocean and the land through processes such as atmosphere–ocean gas transfer and chemical (e.g., weathering) and biological (e.g., photosynthesis) processes. While more than half of the CO_2 emitted is currently removed from the atmosphere within a century, some fraction (about 20%) of emitted CO_2 remains in the atmosphere for many millennia. Because of slow removal processes, atmospheric CO_2 will continue to increase in the long term even if its emission is substantially reduced from present levels." *Climate Change 2007.*

quantities of the same heat-trapping gases that cause the natural greenhouse effect, thereby producing an enhanced greenhouse effect that is increasing the average surface temperature of the planet. Though greatly simplified, this captures the essence of the argument presented by scientists around the world to support the claim that humans have brought about most of the warming of the last century. Indeed, this corresponds to the assertion made by the IPCC of a greater than 95% likelihood that the present warming is caused by increases in the concentration of heat-trapping gases in the atmosphere.[41] There is a less than 5% chance that the present warming is solely caused by "natural variability."

However, this sort of argument often meets with incredulity. Many question whether it is really that certain. They point out that news outlets report on a vigorous and ongoing debate regarding whether climate change is happening and if it is, whether human activities are the cause. Many also argue that scientists have been wrong before, so who is to say that they aren't wrong now?

What If We Are Wrong?

Given the nature of the media coverage of global warming, one might assume significant disagreement among scientists on the question of whether Earth's climate is changing and if it is, what is causing it. However, the public's perception of the state of climate science differs considerably from the actual science. For instance, when Oreskes analyzed 928 peer-reviewed science articles published between 1993 and 2003, she did not find a single article citing evidence contradicting the theory that global climate change is happening and is largely anthropogenic. Contrary to public perception, active climate researchers no longer debate whether climate change is happening or whether human activities cause it. Most research now focuses on understanding how fast it is happening and with what consequences.[42]

---

41. IPCC, *Climate Change 2013*.

42. Naomi Oreskes, "The Scientific Consensus on Climate Change: How Do We Know We're Not Wrong?," in *Climate Change: What It Means for Us, Our Children, and Our Grandchildren*, ed. Joseph F. C. DiMento and Pamela Doughman (Cambridge, MA: MIT Press, 2007), 70–71.

Every subsequent study has confirmed Oreskes's results.[43] For instance, one study, "Examining the Scientific Consensus on Climate Change" conducted in 2009, asked 3,146 scientists two simple questions: "1. When compared with pre-1800s levels, do you think that mean global temperatures have generally risen, fallen, or remained relatively constant? 2. Do you think human activity is a significant contributing factor in changing mean global temperatures?"[44] The results were unambiguous, with 90% of respondents answering "risen" to question 1 and 82% answering "yes" to question 2.[45] Furthermore, analysis of the answers to the second question reveals a clear correlation between a "yes" answer and the depth of the researcher's knowledge about the climate:

> The most specialized and knowledgeable respondents (with regard to climate change) are those who listed climate science as their area of expertise and who also have published more than 50 percent of their recent peer-reviewed papers on the subject of climate change (79 individuals in total). Of these specialists, 96.2 percent (76 of 79) answered "risen" to question 1 and 97.4 percent (75 of 77) answered "yes" to question 2.[46]

For climate scientists, then, the main question is not whether Earth is warming or whether humans are a significant factor in that

---

43. See John Cook et al., "Quantifying the Consensus on Anthropogenic Global Warming in the Scientific Literature," *Environmental Research Letters* (January 18, 2013), doi:10.1088/1748-9326/8/2/024024). "In the most comprehensive analysis performed to date, we have extended the analysis of peer-reviewed climate papers in Oreskes (2004). We examined a large sample of the scientific literature on global CC, published over a 21-year period, in order to determine the level of scientific consensus that human activity is very likely causing most of the current GW (anthropogenic global warming, or AGW). Surveys of climate scientists have found strong agreement (97–98 percent) regarding AGW amongst publishing climate experts (Doran and Zimmerman 2009, Anderegg et al. 2010). Repeated surveys of scientists found that scientific agreement about AGW steadily increased from 1996 to 2009 (Bray 2010). This is reflected in the increasingly definitive statements issued by the Intergovernmental Panel on Climate Change on the attribution of recent GW (Houghton et al. 1996, 2001, Solomon et al. 2007)."

44. Peter T. Doran and Maggie Kendall Zimmerman, "Examining the Scientific Consensus on Climate Change," *Eos* 90, no. 3 (January 2009): 22.

45. Ibid.

46. Ibid.

warming but rather how much and how fast these changes will occur. As Oreskes puts it, "Virtually all professional climate scientists agree on the reality of human-induced climate change, but debate continues on tempo and mode."[47] While considerable disagreement in the scientific literature exists, the debate concerns the speed (tempo) and the exact mechanisms (mode) of the warming, not whether it is taking place or whether human activities are the primary cause.

Climate Change Perception Gap[48]

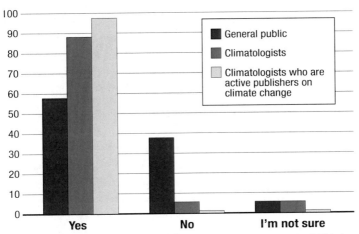

Figure 2.4. Is human activity a significant cause of global warming? This bar graph captures responses from three categories of people to this question.

The growing consilience of scientific evidence demonstrating climate change as human-induced, however, seems to run contrary to public perception. As scientific certainty regarding the anthropogenic climate change increases, public "belief" in human-caused climate change seems to decrease. According to a 2008 Pew Research Center survey in the United States, 47% of respondents answered question 2 affirmatively (compared to 82% of scientists and 97.4% of

47. Oreskes, "Scientific Consensus," 73–74.

48. Chart adapted from Doran and Zimmerman, "Examining the Scientific Consensus," 22–23.

active climate scientists), while in 2010 only 34% agreed that global warming is caused by human activities, a drop of 13 percentage points.[49] Although as of 2014, 44% of respondents acknowledge that Earth's warming is "mostly due to human activity," this still contrasts greatly with the views and research of scientists.[50] Why is the public's perception of the state of the science so dramatically different than the actual state of the science?

False Equivalency, Climate Skepticism, and Denial

In general, the American news media has not paid much attention to climate change. However, when it has, the media has sought to follow the doctrine of fairness, ensuring that "both sides of the debate are equally represented." But should both "sides" of the climate change debate get equal time? According to Oreskes and Conway,

> The simple answer is no. While the idea of equal time for opposing opinions makes sense in a two-party political system, it does not work for science, because science is not about opinion. It is about evidence. It is about claims that can be, and have been, tested through scientific research—experiments, experience, and observation—research that is then subject to *critical review by a jury of scientific peers.* Claims that have not gone through that process—or have gone through it and failed—are not scientific, and do not deserve equal time in a scientific debate.[51]

In science, fairness does not require equal time for unequal views. Science is not democratic and does not consider it "fair" to give equal airtime to a scientific position with a 5% likelihood of being correct as to one with a 95% likelihood of being correct. But this exact

---

49. "Fewer Americans See Solid Evidence of Global Warming," Pew Research Center, October 22, 2009, *http://bit.ly/1nQJZXx*.

50. "Climate Change: Key Data Points from Pew Research," Pew Research Center, January 27, 2014, *http://bit.ly/1f9FUJe*.

51. Oreskes and Conway, *Merchants of Doubt*, 32; emphasis in original.

scenario plays out in the debate over climate change.[52] This is not an instance of "fairness" but one of "false equivalency."

A **false equivalency** is created when two unequal positions are presented as though both were equally plausible. If my theory that a race of shy mole people living below Earth's surface causes earthquakes receives equal airtime with the theory that earthquakes are caused by shifting pieces of Earth's crust (plate tectonics), that would not be an instance of fairness but of false equivalency. Suggesting that my mole person theory deserves equal consideration to that of plate tectonics is not scientifically appropriate. Decades of careful observation and research support the latter, while the former rests on nothing but wild conjecture. Presenting unequal positions equally is not fair; it is misleading.[53] Accurately portraying the issue would require the media to adopt a new model: treating equal positions equally and unequal positions equitably.[54] Every position might deserve a hearing but not necessarily the same amount of airtime.

This leads to one final point regarding the nature of doubt and skepticism and its relationship to science and scientific inquiry. Doubt or healthy skepticism plays a critical role in scientific investigation. Indeed, critically evaluating any position is a mark of an educated person, but there is a difference between healthy skepticism and denial.

---

52. Oreskes and Conway write, "In an active scientific debate, there can be many sides. But once a scientific issue is closed, there's only one 'side.' Imagine providing 'balance' to the issue of whether the Earth orbits the Sun, whether continents move, or whether DNA carries genetic information. These matters were long ago settled in scientists' minds. Nobody can publish an article in a scientific journal claiming the Sun orbits the Earth, and for the same reason, you can't publish an article in a peer-reviewed journal claiming there's no global warming. Probably well-informed professional science journalists wouldn't publish it either. But ordinary journalists repeatedly did." Ibid., 214.

53. "The Fairness Doctrine had been established in the late 1940s, when radio and television licenses were scarce and tightly controlled by the U.S. government. A Federal Communications Commission license was thought to come with an obligation to serve public purposes, one of which was 'fairness.' But does fairness require equal time for unequal views?" Oreskes and Conway, *Merchants of Doubt*, 57.

54. This is an adaptation of a passage from Holmes Rolston III, *Environmental Ethics: Duties to and Values in the Natural World* (Philadelphia: Temple University Press, 1988).

Healthy skepticism is essential to intellectual inquiry. It helps in avoiding dogmatism and unjustified or blind acceptance. It requires one to consider (and even seek) evidence that runs contrary to personal beliefs. The skeptic recognizes her fallibility and finitude and therefore attempts to remain open to the fact that at least some of her positions can and will change over time as new evidence and new arguments are revealed. Whereas skepticism remains essential to intellectual progress and inquiry, denial is corrosive to genuine inquiry because the denier assumes that she already has the truth. She refuses to view or seriously consider evidence or arguments that contradict what she has already accepted as true. Many people have moved past a healthy skepticism toward conclusions of climate science and become climate deniers who refuse to consider any position that contradicts their beliefs. The climate blogger R. L. Miller has coined the provocative term "climate zombies" to refer to such people because they mindlessly go through the world refusing to seriously consider the evidence.[55]

The best climate science today suggests that anthropogenic emissions are extremely likely the cause of the warming. Is it possible that this is wrong? Yes. Scientific research always leaves room for doubt. However, as in a lawsuit, one must ask whether there is reasonable doubt.[56] Oreskes puts this point quite well:

> No scientific conclusion can ever be proven, and new evidence may lead scientists to change their views, but it is no more a "belief" to say that the Earth is heating up than to say that continents move, that germs cause disease, that DNA carries hereditary information, and that HIV causes AIDS. You can always find someone, somewhere, to disagree, but these conclusions represent our best current understandings and therefore our best basis for reasoned action.[57]

Just as in every area of life, people have to do the best they can with their present understanding. Indeed, as the ethicist Dale Jamieson

---

55. "Attack of the Climate Zombies!" *Climate Progress* (blog), September 10, 2010, *http://bit.ly/1kkKlXA*.

56. Oreskes and Conway, *Merchants of Doubt*, 31.

57. Oreskes, "Scientific Consensus," 79.

presciently noted in 1992, it would be dangerously irresponsible to delay action until it is absolutely certain that warming is caused by human activities.

> There are many uncertainties concerning anthropogenic climate change, yet we cannot wait until all the facts are in before we respond. All the facts may never be in. New knowledge may resolve old certainties, but it may bring with it new uncertainties. And it is an important dimension of this problem that our insults to the biosphere outrun our ability to understand them. We may suffer the worst effects of the greenhouse before we can prove to everyone's satisfaction that they will occur.[58]

There seems little choice but to act on the best state of present understanding, with all of the doubt, risk, and messiness that this involves. The point at which one has all the information to make a decision will already be too late. One will never have all the desired information to make important decisions.[59] More study will always be needed, but that does not justify abdicating responsibility to act today on the best state of contemporary understanding.

As the ethicist Stephen Gardiner notes, we should not confuse "uncertainty" and "risk": "In the technical sense, a risk involves a known, or reliably estimable, probability that a certain set of outcomes may occur, whereas an uncertainty arises when such probabilities are not available."[60] Given this technical meaning of uncertainty, it is false to say that there is scientific uncertainty

---

58. Dale Jamieson, "Ethics, Public Policy, and Global Warming," *Science, Technology, & Human Values* 17 (April 1992): 141–42.

59. Environmental science writer Tim Flannery states, "If, for example, we wait to see if an ailment is indeed fatal, we will do nothing until we are dead. Instead, we take medication or whatever else the doctor dispenses, despite the fact that we may survive regardless. And when it comes to more mundane matters, uncertainty hardly deters us: We spend large sums on children's education with no guarantee of a good outcome, and we buy shares with no promise of a return. Excepting death and taxes, certainty does not exist in our world, and yet we often manage our lives in the most efficient manner. I cannot see why our response to climate change should be any different." *Weather Makers*, 7–8.

60. Stephen M. Gardiner, "Ethics and Global Climate Change," in *Climate Ethics: Essential Readings* (Oxford: Oxford University Press, 2010), 7.

surrounding global climate change. We have reliably estimated the likelihood of climate change being anthropogenic; it is extremely likely (>95%). In this way, global warming is a matter of risk, not uncertainty.

Although genuine areas of scientific uncertainty concerning the atmosphere exist,[61] a consilience of evidence makes two conclusions *extremely likely* (>95% likelihood): (1) the atmosphere and oceans are warming at an accelerating rate, and (2) most of this warming is anthropogenic (human-induced). While science can establish whether climate change is happening and its likely cause, it cannot advise humanity how to respond, how to distribute the costs, or what sort of life is worth pursuing. Science cannot ask, much less answer, such questions of meaning and value. Although responsible decision-making remains rooted in science, determining how to live and what to value are ultimately moral questions. The remainder of this volume is dedicated to exploring possible answers to such questions.

For Further Exploration

1. The popular debate over global warming is often full of confusing and contradictory claims. Discerning consumers of media need to know how to separate the "good" from the "bad." This assignment is an example of how you could do that.

   a. Go to the website dedicated to the "Global Warming Petition Project" (formerly called the "Oregon Petition," *www.petition-project.org/*). Once there, browse the related pages. After a thorough surfing, answer the following questions and record your

---

61. Beyond the speed and severity of climate changes, the IPCC describes continuing areas of scientific uncertainty in the following areas: "[1] sources and sinks of greenhouse gases, which affect predictions of future concentrations, [2] clouds, which strongly influence the magnitude of climate change, [3] oceans, which influence the timing and patterns of climate change, [and 4] polar ice-sheets, which affect predictions of sea level rise. These processes are already partially understood, and we are confident that the uncertainties can be reduced by further research. However, the complexity of the system means that we cannot rule out surprises." Houghton, *Global Warming*, 262.

findings in your notes, being careful not to simply accept the obvious answers given by the website. Use websites of organizations such as SourceWatch and other Internet quality control sites to vet information.

- What organization(s) sponsor the Petition Project?
- Using the analysis given by the Petition Project ("qualifications of signers"), what percentage of signatories have expertise in climate science?
- Randomly pick five names of individuals who have signed the petition, some with a PhD and some without. (Consider picking some names that are less common so as to make the next step a bit easier.) Using Google or another search engine, search for each individual. Once you are reasonably sure you have found a website on the individual, write down a brief description of his or her qualifications. If you can't find the person after looking hard, then note that you couldn't find any information on them.

b. Do a series of searches to find out what critics have said about "debunking" the "fallacies" of the global warming petition project. Take notes on what you find. This is a test of your research ability. Keep in mind that part of the task is to figure out how to know what to trust online.

c. Finally, summarize your findings. What did you learn from this process?

2. Explore the difference between healthy skepticism and denial. Visit the website for Skeptical Science (*www.skepticalscience.com*). After browsing the website, pick one skeptical argument that you are most interested in examining more closely (e.g., global warming is caused by changes in radiation from the Sun). Then, find someone in the world who believes this position (do a general Web search). Record the URL, the author, his or her qualifications, and basic position. Return to Skeptical Science and read their view on the topic you've chosen. Which position do you find to be more convincing and why? Was the position you researched that of a skeptic or a denier? Why?

Additional Resources

WEBSITES

Carbon Dioxide Information Analysis Center (CDIAC), *http:// cdiac.ornl.gov/pns/current_ghg.html*

For current atmospheric concentrations of all greenhouse gases.

CO_2 Now, *www.co2now.org/*

For current atmospheric concentrations of all greenhouse gases.

The Consensus Project, *http://theconsensusproject.com/*

The Consensus Project measured the level of consensus in published, peer-reviewed climate research that humans are causing global warming. In the most comprehensive analysis to date, the Project analyzed 21 years' worth of peer-reviewed papers on "global warming" or "global climate change." Among the 12,465 papers, over 4,014 abstracts authored by 10,188 scientists stated a position on human-caused global warming. Among those 4,014 abstracts, 97.1% endorse the consensus. Among the 10,188 scientists, 98.4% endorse the consensus.

Intergovernmental Panel on Climate Change (IPCC), *www.ipcc.ch/*

The IPCC is the leading scientific body worldwide studying climate change. Its reports are the most authoritative statements available. Its "Summary for Policymakers" documents are written in clear and accessible language that is understandable by non-scientists. See, specifically,

- IPCC's Fifth Assessment Report, *www.climatechange 2013.org/*
- Interactive time line of the IPCC and its work, *http://unfccc .int/timeline/*

Pew Research Center, *http://www.pewresearch.org/*

For information on the current views of the public regarding the existence, cause, or importance of climate change. A simple search on Pew's website will bring you to the latest polling data on global warming.

Skeptical Science, *www.skepticalscience.com*

Seeks to explain the results of peer-reviewed climate science to non-scientists. Much of its website is dedicated to responding to common "climate myths," such as the myth that global warming is caused by the Sun, not human-generated gases that trap heat. Skeptical Science has also created mobile apps to make their arguments available via mobile devices (*http://skepticalscience.com/software.shtml*). The website also has a helpful "Climate Science Glossary" (*http://skepticalscience.com/glossary.php*).

Yale Project on Climate Change Communication, *http://environment.yale.edu/climate-communication/*

Conducts research on public climate knowledge, risk perceptions, decision-making, and behavior. Through their research they seek to empower educators and communicators with the knowledge and tools to more effectively engage the public.

BOOKS AND ARTICLES

Broome, John. "A Philosopher at the IPCC." International Society for Environmental Ethics, May 20, 2014, *http://bit.ly/RxDr59*.

An illuminating inside account of how the IPCC goes about writing its summary for policymakers.

Cook, John, et al. "Quantifying the Consensus on Anthropogenic Global Warming in the Scientific Literature." *Environmental Research Letters* (January 18, 2013), doi:10.1088/1748-9326/8/2/024024).

Doran, Peter T., and Maggie Kendall Zimmerman. "Examining the Scientific Consensus on Climate Change." *Eos* 90, no. 3 (January 2009): 22.

Houghton, John. *Global Warming: The Complete Briefing.* 4th ed. Cambridge: Cambridge University Press, 2009.

Written by the founding co-chair of the IPCC, this is one of the most helpful and accessible textbooks on the science of global climate change. It is especially well suited for non-scientists wanting to understand the science behind climate change.

Oreskes, Naomi. "The Scientific Consensus on Climate Change: How Do We Know We're Not Wrong?" In *Climate Change: What It Means for Us, Our Children, and Our Grandchildren*, edited by Joseph F. C. DiMento and Pamela Doughman, 70–71. Cambridge, MA: MIT Press, 2007.

Oreskes, Naomi, and Erik M. Conway. *Merchants of Doubt: How a Handful of Scientists Obscured the Truth on Issues from Tobacco Smoke to Global Warming*. New York: Bloomsbury Press, 2010.

The authors construct a detailed and articulate analysis of the powerful negative effects when industry scientists create campaigns to systematically mislead the public on issues such as the health effects of smoking tobacco and the science of global climate change.

3

CHAPTER

The Political Response to a Changing Climate

The Market-Based Approach

Given the scope and likely causes of global climate change, what ought to be done in response to this grave challenge? This question marks the transition from science, which explains what is happening, to ethics and politics, which discuss why, how, and for what end(s) people should act. As climate ethicist Dale Jamieson has noted,

> The problem we face is not a purely scientific problem that can be solved by the accumulation of scientific information. Science has alerted us to a problem, but the problem also concerns our values. It is about how we ought to live, and how humans should relate to each other and to the rest of nature. These are problems of ethics and politics as well as problems of science.[1]

This chapter considers political efforts to address climate change, focusing in particular on the role of the United States. The subsequent chapters will consider the ethical dimensions underlying these efforts.

---

1. Dale Jamieson, "Ethics, Public Policy, and Global Warming," in *Climate Ethics: Essential Readings*, ed. Stephen M. Gardiner et al. (Oxford: Oxford University Press, 2010), 142.

The International Political Process: Rio, Kyoto, and Beyond

Dating the birth of a movement is always difficult. Ideas are "in the air" long before they achieve widespread public attention. This is true of environmentalism. For many scholars the origins of the American environmental movement date back to the writings and work of people such as John Muir (1838–1914), Gifford Pinchot (1865–1946), and Aldo Leopold (1887–1948).[2] In the 1920s, efforts such as theirs inspired the "conservation movement," which in turn led to the creation of the first national parks and monuments. The modern environmental movement, which went beyond the conservation movement by addressing issues such as air and water pollution, began to grow in earnest in the 1960s, thanks to books such as *Silent Spring* (1962) by Rachel Carson, which exposed the harm done by insecticides such as DDT. Environmentalism reached national prominence with the celebration of the first Earth Day on April 22, 1970. For many people, the message of Earth Day was best captured by the images of Earth taken from space on December 7, 1972 (see fig. 3.1). This photograph—arguably the most widely distributed picture ever taken—revealed both the beauty and the fragility of the planet.

By the 1980s, the environmental movement's ideas had become central to the work of the United Nations and its World Commission on Environment and Development. This commission is commonly called the Brundtland Commission, after its chair, Gro Harlem Brundtland. Moving beyond concerns regarding pollution, the commission focused on defining the idea of "sustainable development." In its final report in 1987, it concluded that sustainable development should "become a central guiding principle of the United Nations, Governments and private institutions, organizations and enterprises."[3]

The international community's response to climate change began in earnest in 1992 when more than 160 countries signed

---

2. For a more complete discussion of the history of the environmental movement, see Eugene Hargrove, "The Historical Foundations of American Environmental Attitudes," *Environmental Ethics* 1 (1979): 209–40.

3. United Nations General Assembly, 96th Plenary Meeting, *Report of the World Commission on Environment and Development*, A/RES/42/187, December 11, 1987.

© pio3./Shutterstock.com

Figure 3.1. These views of Earth from space are digitally combined from a series of photos taken from Apollo 17 in December 1972.

the **United Nations Framework Convention on Climate Change (UNFCCC)** at the Rio Earth Summit, held in Rio de Janeiro, Brazil. The ultimate goal of the convention was to stabilize concentrations of greenhouse gases "at a level which would prevent dangerous anthropogenic interference with the climate system."[4]

At the Rio meeting, many wealthy nations, including the United States, Canada, Japan, and the European Union, agreed to voluntarily stabilize their annual emissions at 1990 levels by 2000.[5] Despite these commitments, emissions continued to rise among nearly all nations, and it quickly became clear that the voluntary measures agreed to in Rio were insufficient. Thus the countries that had ratified the UNFCCC agreed to meet in Berlin, Germany, in 1995 to develop a specific protocol regarding binding emissions reductions. This meeting in Berlin marked the first of what has become an annual **Conference of the Parties (COP)** to the Climate Convention.[6] The treaty was finalized two years later in Kyoto, Japan, with the successful negotiation of the Kyoto Protocol.

4. "Article 2," *Rio Declaration on Environment and Development,* United Nations Environment Programme, *http://bit.ly/1jqNrnN.*

5. Stephen M. Gardiner, "Ethics and Global Climate Change," in *Climate Ethics: Essential Readings,* ed. Stephen M. Gardiner et al. (Oxford: Oxford University Press, 2010), 19.

6. Since the first meeting in Berlin in 1995, a Conference of the Parties has been held every year, with two held in 2001.

The Kyoto Protocol sought to reduce emissions by having the richer, industrialized nations take the lead, while poorer, developing nations would focus on growing their economies and pulling their people out of poverty. The proposed division between richer countries and poorer countries would last for an initial commitment period until 2012, after which all nations would be required to mitigate their emissions. This model, sometimes referred to as "contraction and convergence," asks developed nations to contract (reduce) their emissions, converging at a lower point with the emissions of developing nations. At that point, all nations would begin to reduce their emissions (see fig. 3.2).

Due in part to US prompting, international leaders designed the Kyoto Protocol as a "market-based" approach to emission reduction. It seeks to create economic disincentives for using carbon-intensive

Contraction and Convergence

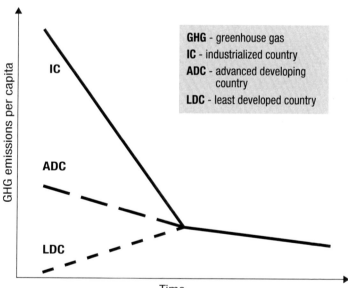

Figure 3.2. This graph depicts the structure of the Kyoto Protocol. In the first phase the least developed countries grow their economies (increasing emissions), while more developed countries "contract" their emissions until they "converge" with the emissions of the least developed countries. After convergence all nations reduce emissions.

forms of energy and transportation (especially coal and oil) while creating economic incentives for lower-carbon forms (e.g., solar, wind, geothermal, tidal, and biomass). Although this strategy can be pursued in several ways, the centerpiece of this approach is the creation of a "cap and trade" system, according to which the international community sets a limit or cap on the amount of carbon dioxide equivalent (CO_2e; a metric for measuring greenhouse gas emissions) that may be emitted. Shares of this cap are then allocated (or sold) to the various stakeholders, such as electricity utilities. These shares or emission permits allow the stakeholder to release a certain quantity of greenhouse gases. If a stakeholder creates less pollution than their shares allow, it can sell the excess emission credits on a special trading market to those who have exceeded their allowance. For instance, if a photovoltaic solar array creates electricity with little or no release of CO_2, it can sell its excess credits to coal-fired power plants that release large quantities of CO_2. Thus by putting a price on greenhouse gas pollution, this market-based cap and trade system creates economic incentives for adopting less-polluting ways of doing business.

Although the United States was a signatory to the Kyoto Protocol (vice president Al Gore signed the treaty), the US Senate never ratified it. In fact, senators from both parties unanimously rejected the treaty. The refusal of the United States to ratify the treaty proved a devastating blow to the fledgling international process. For the protocol to become legally binding in international law, two conditions had to be met: (1) at least 55 nations had to ratify the protocol, and (2) the total emissions of developed nations ratifying the treaty must represent at least 55% of all emissions from developed nations.[7] Given this high bar and the fact that the United States contributed such a large share of global emissions (36% in 1990), most considered the protocol dead when the Bush administration officially announced withdrawal from the protocol in 2001. However, despite many setbacks, with Russia's ratification in 2004, the Protocol passed the 55% emissions threshold, and therefore the protocol came into legal force on February 16, 2005, only seven years before its first phase was set to conclude.[8] Though the Kyoto Protocol did provide

---

7. John Houghton, *Global Warming: The Complete Briefing*, 4th ed. (Cambridge: Cambridge University Press, 2009), 297.

8. Ibid., 295.

significant momentum for the creation of a cap and trade market in the EU and could reasonably claim to have brought about some emission reductions, as the centerpiece of the international political efforts to address climate change, the protocol has not lived up to its promise. The reasons for this are complex, but a significant reason for the failure of the protocol is because the largest source of emissions, the United States, was not covered by the treaty. However, the rise of globalism (and in particular the rise of China's economy) is also a significant factor in the failure of the protocol.[9]

Kyoto and Its US Critics

The bipartisan rejection of the Kyoto Protocol by the US Senate stemmed in large part from the Byrd-Hagel Resolution, which mandated that any international agreement addressing climate change must require all nations, both developed and developing, to reduce emissions and must not "result in serious harm to the economy of the United States."[10] This resolution, which unanimously passed (95–0) in July 1997, captures the two main objections to both the Kyoto Protocol in particular and international efforts to curb greenhouse gas emissions in general. In essence, critics of the Protocol object (1) that requiring developed nations but not developing nations to curb their emissions is unfair[11] and (2) that reducing carbon pollution will hurt the US economy.

Fair Is Fair?

In the second of three televised debates between (then Texas governor) George W. Bush and vice president Al Gore during the 2000 presidential campaign, Bush was asked about his views on climate change. He replied, "I'll tell you one thing I'm not going to do is I'm not going to let the United States carry the burden for cleaning up the world's air,

---

9. For a comprehensive discussion of the failure of international climate change mitigation efforts, see Dale Jamieson, *Reason in a Dark Time: Why the Struggle against Climate Change Failed—And What It Means for Our Future* (Oxford: Oxford University Press, 2014).

10. Byrd-Hagel Resolution, S. Res. 98, 105th Cong. (1997), National Center for Public Policy Research, *www.nationalcenter.org/KyotoSenate.html*.

11. Many critics fail to note that this was only to be the case for the initial commitment period, after which all nations would have to reduce their emissions.

like the Kyoto treaty would have done. China and India were exempted from that treaty. I think we need to be more even-handed."[12] This reference to even-handedness reflects the objection to requiring developed nations to reduce their emissions while not requiring the same of developing nations. Does fairness, however, require the same standards for all countries? Might it be fair to ask developed nations to reduce their emissions while allowing developing nations to continue to grow their economy and their emissions, at least for a period of time?

Princeton University ethicist Peter Singer notes several different ways of understanding fairness in this context. According to a "historical principle" of fairness, "we can't decide merely by looking at the present situation whether a given distribution of goods is just or unjust. We must also ask how the situation came about; we must know its history."[13] On the other hand, one might use a "time-slice principle" of fairness, which "looks at the existing distribution at a particular moment and asks if that distribution satisfies some principles of fairness, irrespective of any preceding sequence of events."[14] Though these distinctions might sound complicated, most children apply them quite naturally. Indeed, my two young daughters often employ one or both of these principles in their squabbling. Imagine that I enter the dining room to find a mess of paper, crayons, pencils, markers, and other art supplies on the table. If I ask both of my daughters to help clean up, my younger daughter might object, noting that she did not create the mess and therefore should not be asked to help clean it up. She is appealing to a historical principle of fairness, in that she looks to the past (who created the mess?) to determine present responsibility. On the other hand, my older daughter, who made the mess, would object to her sister being excused, suggesting that everyone should pitch in to clean up the mess, regardless of who created it. My older daughter is appealing to a time-slice principle of fairness, in that she advises ignoring the past (who did it?) and looking only at present circumstances to determine responsibility.

---

12. Quoted in Peter Singer, "One Atmosphere," in *Climate Ethics: Essential Readings,* ed. Stephen M. Gardiner et al. (Oxford: Oxford University Press, 2010), 187. Note that China and India were not "exempted." Rather, as developing countries, they had different responsibilities in the first commitment period than the United States and other developed countries.

13. Ibid.

14. Ibid.

There are several ways to refine this time-slice model of fairness. For instance, one might apportion responsibility equally, suggesting that everyone bear an equal burden. Or one might assign responsibility based on ability to help. With the example of the art supplies, according to the "equal share" version, everyone should pick up exactly the same amount. On the other hand, the "ability to help" version would require each person to pick up according to their ability to do so. My daughters would happily agree that that would mean I should pick up most of the mess!

Given these various ways of understanding fairness, are former President Bush and other critics of the Kyoto Protocol correct in suggesting that the Protocol is unfair (not "even-handed")? The leaders of most developing nations contend that because the developed nations both caused and benefited from global warming, the developed nations should in turn do more to solve the problem. In many ways, the designers of the Kyoto Protocol based it on a historical principle of fairness, what some refer to as the "polluter pays" model. In its first commitment period, the protocol required developed nations to reduce their emissions on the principle that these nations created the pollution changing the climate and benefited from the wealth created by this industrialization. Thus the Kyoto Protocol is "even-handed" on a historical principle of fairness.

However, what about a time-slice model of fairness? After all, only recently (since perhaps 1990) have scientists understood the full implications of releasing large quantities of CO_2 into the atmosphere. Therefore, one could argue that the developed nations should not be held accountable for emissions released during the last 150 years, since the start of the Industrial Revolution. Instead, according to a time-slice principle of fairness, nations should look at the present instead of the past when apportioning responsibility. Again, this time-slice principle could be interpreted on an equal share, per-capita basis or on the "ability to help" model.

With the latter model, one should be expected to "clean up the mess" according to ability. Considering that developed nations are wealthier than developing nations, defenders of the Kyoto Protocol contend that developed nations should do more. Indeed, one could argue, given that the US economy constitutes more than 20% of the world economy, that the United States should bear one-fifth the cost of addressing climate change. This would be "even-handed" based on an "ability to help," time-slice principle of fairness.

Instead of making calculations based on the ability to help, what if the costs of using the global atmosphere were distributed equally, per capita? According to the World Bank the average American creates 17.6 metric tons of CO_2 annually, whereas the average Chinese is responsible for only 6.2 metric tons, and the average Indian only 1.7 metric tons.[15] On an "equal share" time-slice principle, these figures suggest Americans should reduce their emissions far more than people in developing nations such as China or India.[16] Thus both a historical principle of fairness and an "equal share" or "ability to help" version of the time-slice principle justifies the Kyoto Protocol's different requirements for developed and developing nations.

In light of this, it would seem that the first concern embodied in the Byrd-Hagel Resolution is unfounded; it *is* fair that developed nations take the lead in addressing the climate change they caused. Despite this, in the interest of developing an international policy acceptable to the United States, the international community has begun to move away from the division between developed and developing countries. As the 2012 expiration of the first phase of the Kyoto Protocol neared, negotiations for the planned second phase between the developed nations and developing nations broke down. However, in a series of meetings between 2010 and 2015, a new framework began to take shape. In particular, the COP meetings in Cancun, Mexico (2010), and Durban, South Africa (2011), created a sort of bridge to serve as the basis for a new international response to climate change (see table 3.1). The key innovation consisted of abandoning the Kyoto Protocol's division between developed and developing nations. If ratified, this

---

15. These figures come from the World Bank for 2010, "CO_2 Emissions," *http://bit.ly/1h4shNk* and only take into consideration CO_2, not other greenhouse gases, such as methane and nitrous oxide.

16. Singer states, "One objection to this approach is that allowing countries to have allocations based on the number of people gives them insufficient incentive to do anything about population growth. . . . By setting allocations that are tied to a specified population, rather than allowing national allocations to rise with an increase in national population, we can meet this objection. We could fix the allocation on the country's population in a given year, say 1990, or the year that the agreement comes into force." "One Atmosphere," 191.

new framework would cover 100% of global emissions, although the new treaty would not take effect until 2020 at the earliest.[17]

TABLE 3.1		
Summary of Agreements Key to a New Climate Change International Framework for Mitigating Climate Change[18]		
Kyoto Protocol	**Cancun Agreements**	**The Durban Platform**
Adopted: 1997 **Reauthorized:** 2011	**Adopted:** 2010 **Expires:** 2020	**Adopted:** 2011, to be completed in 2015 with goal to enter into force in 2020
Total emissions covered: 42% in 1990, 27% in 2008, 15% in 2011	**Total emissions covered:** 80% based on submissions of plans by developed and developing countries	**Total emissions covered:** 100%
Targets: Binding only for developed countries, 5.2% below 1990 emission levels to 2012	**Targets:** Non-binding but aims to keep world on 2°C stabilization pathway	**Targets:** Still being negotiated

As Andrew Light, professor of philosophy and public policy and director of the Institute for Philosophy and Public Policy at George Mason University,[19] explained, "The firewall between developed and

---

17. Andrew Light et al., "Doha Climate Summit Ends with the Long March to 2015," Center for American Progress, December 11, 2012, *http://bit.ly/1mlVoO5*.

18. This table is adapted from "The Bridge to the Durban Outcome," a visualization created by the Center for America Progress, *http://bit.ly/1ioKCUx*.

19. Light is currently on leave from his academic post and is serving as a senior adviser to the special envoy on climate change in the US Department of State. Andrew Light, George Mason University, Institute for Philosophy and Public Policy, *http://ippp.gmu.edu/people/light.html*.

developing countries is gone. The Durban Platform was built explicitly on the promise that the framework convention would not again produce a treaty that was not symmetrical, applying to all parties under the Convention."[20] Though it may have been fair to expect greater emission reductions from wealthier countries, erasing the division between developing and developed countries eliminates a key objection that has undermined international climate negotiations for nearly two decades. The chief remaining concern of those who are against taking aggressive action to address climate change is that any effort to reduce greenhouse gas emissions would harm the US economy.

Abbreviated Time Line of International Efforts to Address Climate Change

1990	First Assessment Report of the Intergovernmental Panel on Climate Change (IPCC) published
1992	Rio Earth Summit, United Nations Framework Convention on Climate Change
1995	The first Conference of the Parties to the Climate Convention, Berlin
1997	US Senate passes the Byrd-Hagel Resolution 95-0
2001	United States withdraws from Kyoto Protocol
2005	Kyoto Protocol becomes legally binding
2010	Cancun Agreements
2011	"Durban Bridge" agreed on for Kyoto Protocol successor
2014	IPCC's Fifth Assessment Report published
2015	Planned successor to Kyoto Protocol submitted for ratification[21]

---

20. Andrew Light, "Why Durban Matters: International Climate Process Strengthened at South Africa Talks," *Center for American Progress*, December 19, 2011, *http://bit.ly/1ioKCUx*.

21. For an interactive time line of the IPCC and its work, see "UNFCCC: 20 Years of Effort and Achievement," United Nations Framework Convention on Climate Change, *http://unfccc.int/timeline/*.

Is It Affordable?

For perhaps understandable reasons, the objection that reducing greenhouse gas pollution will hurt the economy (whether the US economy or the global economy) has become the dominant argument against significant action on climate change. For decades, opponents of environmental regulation (both in the United States and internationally) have pitted economic prosperity against environmental protection. These critics have led the public to believe they must choose either economic prosperity or environmental protection.

For instance, US car manufacturers have long opposed government regulation requiring increases in the fuel efficiency of cars because they claim it will increase vehicle prices and, in turn, decrease sales and profits. This will lead to auto worker layoffs and hurt the economy. They suggest consumers must choose between cleaner air and affordable cars and factory jobs. Despite these objections, in 2011 the Obama administration successfully advocated for higher vehicle efficiency requirements—referred to as CAFE or Corporate Average Fuel Efficiency standards—from a target of 35.5 miles per gallon (mpg) in 2016 to 54.5 mpg by 2025. These requirements are expected to save 12 billion barrels of oil during the life of the program, avoiding the release of 6 billion metric tons (6.6 billion tons) of CO_2. Although incorporating the efficiency technologies will increase the price of each vehicle by $800, it is expected that consumers will *save* $1.7 trillion dollars in fuel during the life of the program.

According to the British economist Nicholas Stern, suggesting that consumers must choose between responsible economic decisions and a clean, stable environment sets up a **false dichotomy**. He further argues that the international failure to address global climate change "must be regarded as market failure on the greatest scale the world has seen."[22] Making sense of this claim requires an understanding of what economists call **externalities** or costs associated with a product or process that are not reflected in the price the consumer pays. Economists find externalities problematic because they

---

22. Nicholas Stern, *The Economics of Climate Change: The Stern Review* (Cambridge: Cambridge University Press, 2007), 27.

distort the market; consumers pay less at the point of sale than a product actually costs. However, these costs, though perhaps ignored, do not disappear. They are paid but often by society at large.

The price of a pack of cigarettes, for example, reflects the costs of growing, picking, drying, and processing the tobacco, as well as the costs of bringing it to market and marketing it to consumers. The consumer's price includes all of these costs, plus taxes and whatever profit margins are added by the various intermediaries along the way. However, some externalities associated with smoking are not reflected in the cost. For instance, smokers have higher incidents of heart disease and various forms of cancer, as do nonsmokers who are exposed to secondhand smoke. Treating these conditions is not only costly to the patient but also increases insurance costs for everyone, as medical insurance premiums are based on a distribution of the overall costs of claims. These economic externalities (e.g., health-care costs or lost productivity due to illness) are real and often significant, but the retail price the consumer pays does not reflect them. For the economist, this represents a "market failure." A market-based approach to such a problem would create mechanisms to "internalize" the economic externalities, thereby eliminating or mitigating the price distortions. In essence, "internalizing the externalities" is the economists' way of saying that the price of a pack of cigarettes should reflect its true cost, including the expense of medical problems that may arise later. Internalizing these costs will make the product more expensive, which will in turn moderate the rate of consumption and the negative effects. Indeed, lawmakers of many states have based their decisions to levy an additional tax on each pack of cigarettes on this logic.

This understanding of market failures and externalities helps place Stern's claim in its larger context:

> The climate is a public good: those who fail to pay for it cannot be excluded from enjoying its benefits and one person's enjoyment of the climate does not diminish the capacity of others to enjoy it too. Markets do not automatically provide the right type of quantity of public goods, because in the absence of public policy there are limited

or no returns to private investors for doing so: in this case, markets for relevant goods and services (energy, land use, innovation, etc.) do not reflect the consequences of different consumption and investment choices for the climate. Thus, climate change is an example of market failure involving externalities and public goods. . . . All in all, it must be regarded as market failure on the greatest scale the world has seen.[23]

Understanding how climate change represents a market failure requires a more precise sense of the externalities involved in the case of global warming. Burning coal to produce electricity serves as a case in point. At present, coal ranks among the cheapest forms of energy not only because it is often heavily subsidized (another distortion of the market) but also because the price of coal does not factor in many of the costs associated with it. The price of a ton of coal reflects the costs of mining and transportation but omits the very real costs to human health and the environment that come with burning it.

Many studies have shown that the emissions released from burning coal contain sulfur and nitrogen oxides, which can lead to asthma, cardiac disease, and cancer. They also contain mercury, which contaminates ground water and has neurological effects similar to that of lead.[24] A study by the American Lung Association estimates that pollution from coal-fired power plants kills 13,000 Americans each year.[25] As in the case of smoking cigarettes, these health costs are externalities. They are not reflected in the price utility companies pay for a ton of coal or that consumers pay for the electricity generated from it.

More relevant to climate change, burning coal also releases large quantities of CO_2 into the atmosphere. In the United States, burning coal provides about 40% of electricity generation, but it represents

---

23. Stern, *Economics of Climate Change*, 27.

24. Alex Gabbard, "Coal Combustion: Nuclear Resource or Danger," last modified February 5, 2008, *http://1.usa.gov/1jY7Q8e*.

25. American Lung Association, "Toxic Air: Time to Clean Up Coal-fired Power Plants," March 8, 2011, *www.lung.org/about-us/our-impact/top-stories/toxic-air-coal-fired-power-plants.html*.

the single largest source of CO_2 emissions.[26] CO_2 is a potent greenhouse gas, contributing to increases in the global average surface temperature by trapping more heat at Earth's surface. The many changes to the climate caused by global warming result in significant economic costs.

For instance, in their survey of economic reports on the projected US costs associated with climate change this century, the Center for Integrative Environmental Research at the University of Maryland found that climate change will affect "all sectors of the [US] economy—most notably agriculture, energy, and transportation."[27] In the western and northwestern United States, climate change will alter precipitation and snow patterns, greatly increasing the risk of forest fires and the significant economic costs associated with fighting them.

> Forest fires cost billions of dollars to suppress and can result in significant loss of property. The Oakland, California fire of 1991 and the fires in San Diego and San Bernardino Counties in 2003 each cost over $2 billion. Every year for the past four years, over 7 million acres of forest in the National Forest System have burned with annual suppression costs of $1.3 billion or more.[28]

The Great Plains and the Midwest will likely experience increased frequency and severity of both flooding and drought, which will cause "billions of dollars in damages to crops and property. For example, the North Dakota Red River floods in 1997 caused $1 billion in agricultural production losses, and the Midwest floods of 1993 inflicted $6–8 billion in damages to farmers alone."[29] New England and the Mid-Atlantic coastal states can continue to expect more severe storms and damage caused by rising sea level: "Since 1980,

---

26. John M. Broder, "E.P.A. Will Delay Rule Limiting Carbon Emissions at New Power Plants," *New York Times*, April 12, 2013, *http://nyti.ms/TR3Vkf*.

27. Matthias Ruth, Dana Coelho, Daria Karetnikov, *The US Economic Impacts of Climate Change and the Costs of Inaction* (College Park: University of Maryland, 2007), 3, *http://bit.ly/ScplH7*.

28. Ibid.

29. Ibid., 3–4.

there have been 70 natural weather-caused disasters, with damages to coastal infrastructure exceeding $1 billion per event. Taken together, their combined impact surpassed $560 billion in damages."[30] Finally, the South and Southwest will likely experience even more strain on already low freshwater levels, which will greatly impact agriculture. For instance, "net agricultural income for the San Antonio, Texas, Edwards Aquifer region is predicted to decline by 16–29% by 2030 and by 30–45% by 2090 because of competing uses for an increasingly scarce resource—water."[31]

It is because of these significant economic externalities (e.g., costs of responding to larger, more frequent storms; costs of failed or flooded crops; costs of fires), Stern argues, that climate change represents a fundamental market failure. The market has failed to reflect all the attendant costs in the price of a ton of coal or a barrel of oil. Economists suggest internalizing those costs by putting a price on carbon pollution.[32] If the costs associated with carbon pollution released by burning coal were internalized, a ton of coal would likely cost more than the number of wind turbines or photovoltaic cells required to create a comparable amount of energy.

The philosopher Henry Shue points out that a market-based approach—internalizing economic externalities and using market forces to incentivize lower-carbon forms of energy and transportation—differs little from what parents require of their children:

> All over the world parents teach their children to clean up their own messes. This simple rule makes good sense from the point of view of incentive: if one learns that one will not be allowed to get away with simply walking away from whatever messes one creates, one is given a strong negative incentive against making messes in the first place. . . . Economists have glorified this simple rule as the "Internalization of externalities." If the basis for the

---

30. Ibid., 4.

31. Ibid.

32. See, for instance, Stern, *Economics of Climate Change*; and Organisation for Economic Co-operation and Development, *Climate and Carbon: Aligning Prices and Policies* (October 9, 2013), *www.oecd.org/greengrowth/climate-carbon.htm*.

price of a product does not incorporate the costs of cleaning up the mess made in the process of producing the product, the costs are being externalized; that is, dumped upon other parties. Incorporating into the basis of the price of the product the costs that had been coercively socialized is called internalizing an externality.[33]

Putting a price on carbon—whether through a carbon tax or through a "cap and trade" approach such as outlined in the Kyoto Protocol—would enlist normal market forces to move the global economy toward cleaner forms of energy and transportation. For instance, if consumers paid the true economic cost associated with pumping, refining, and burning oil, they would likely spend more than $10 per gallon of gasoline. If the military cost of securing the oil were included, the price would run still higher. Paying the true cost for gasoline would encourage consumers to buy more efficient cars, drive less, and demand better public transportation. A market reflecting the true cost of carbon-intensive forms of energy would likely result in a dramatic shift toward low-carbon forms of energy production and transportation.

However, internalizing externalities associated with carbon-intensive forms of energy would decrease the profits of the some of the largest, most profitable corporations in the world. As environmentalist and author Bill McKibben explains,

> The five biggest oil companies have made more than $1 trillion in profits since the millennium—there's simply too much money to be made on oil and gas and coal to go chasing after zephyrs and sunbeams. Much of that profit stems from a single historical accident: alone among businesses, the fossil-fuel industry is allowed to dump its waste, carbon dioxide, for free. Nobody else gets that break—if you own a restaurant, you have to pay someone to cart away your trash, since piling it in the street would breed rats. But

---

33. Henry Shue, "Global Environment and International Inequity," in *Climate Ethics: Essential Readings*, ed. Stephen M. Gardiner et al. (Oxford: Oxford University Press, 2010), 103.

the fossil-fuel industry is different, and for sound historical reasons: Until a quarter-century ago, almost no one knew that CO_2 was dangerous. But now that we understand that carbon is heating the planet and acidifying our oceans, its price becomes the central issue.[34]

It would seem, then, that the second objection embodied in the Byrd-Hagel Resolution—that addressing climate change will hurt the economy—is mistaken. Contrary to critics' claims, most economists argue that international treaties such as the Kyoto Protocol will not hurt either the US economy or the global economy but rather force them to more accurately reflect the true cost of carbon-intensive forms of transportation and energy production. According to the Organisation for Economic Co-operation and Development (OECD), "Policy action [on climate change] is affordable, and the cost of inaction is high."[35] Indeed, the longer nations defer action on climate change, the more severe the expected repercussions are (see chap. 1) and the more expensive the remediation.[36] As the OECD explains,

> Meeting the environmental challenges is both economically rational and technologically feasible. Seen from a long-term perspective, the costs of early action are far less than the costs of delaying; the earlier we act, the easier and less expensive the task will be. Policy-makers, businesses and consumers all need to play their part to implement the ambitious policy reforms which will deliver the most cost-effective environmental improvements. In that way, options are left open for future generations to make their own choices about how to enhance their well-being.[37]

---

34. Bill McKibben, "Global Warming's Terrifying New Math," *Rolling Stone*, July 19, 2012, *http://rol.st/1bYUwIk*.

35. *OECD Environmental Outlook to 2030: Executive Summary*, Organisation for Economic Co-operation and Development, 2008, 7, *http://bit.ly/Scpx9r*.

36. See Intergovernmental Panel on Climate Change, *Climate Change 2014: Mitigation of Climate Change*, 2014, *http://mitigation2014.org/report/*.

37. *OECD Environmental Outlook to 2030*, 13.

However, what if the rate of climate change is not as swift as predicted or the costs not as high? What if governments around the globe price carbon pollution (through a carbon tax or cap and trade program) and shift large sectors of the economy toward new forms of energy and transportation, only to find that climate change is not as severe as predicted? A cartoon published in *USA Today* in 2009, just before the COP met in Copenhagen to negotiate a successor to the Kyoto Protocol, captures this sentiment well (see fig. 3.3).

> If (as is unlikely) the risks of high concentrations turn out to be low and we have taken action, we would still have purchased a cleaner, more biodiverse, and more attractive world, at modest cost. If our actions are weak and the central scientific estimates are correct, we will be in very dangerous circumstances, from which it may be impossible, or very costly, to recover.[38]

Figure 3.3. In 2009, just before the Climate Change Conference in Copenhagen, this Joel Pett cartoon appeared in USA Today.

---

38. Stern, *Economics of Climate Change*, 45.

Outsourcing Morality to Economics?

Although a careful economic analysis undermines the claim that supporting international efforts to address climate change would hurt the economy, this belies a more fundamental question: does economics alone provide an adequate basis for defining how human beings should relate to the natural world?[39] Are there some values which in principle cannot be captured adequately by economics? For instance, can economics adequately reflect the loss of one's nation due to encroaching sea water (as has happened to the Carteret Islanders)? In principle, can economics adequately capture what is lost in the extinction of a species? Is climate change just an economic problem to be fixed by building a more perfect market? Does it *merely* represent a "market failure" or an engineering problem to be solved with the deployment of the latest "green" technologies? Ethicists argue that the issues raised by climate change move the discussion beyond questions of economics to ones of fundamental value.

As ethicist Dale Jamieson points out, an accounting of the costs and benefits of different courses of action is important: "It would be wrong and foolish to deny the importance of economic information."[40] However, problems arise when economic efficiency is the *only* value considered. Thus, as Jamieson indicates, thinking of global climate change as merely a problem to be managed is a "dangerous conceit."[41] Not only are the "tools of economic evaluation . . . not up to the task," but economic evaluation prescribes a "medicine" that is, in fact, the cause of the disease.[42] Jamieson diagnoses the problem with this approach:

> The most fundamental reason why management approaches are doomed to failure is that the questions they can answer are not the ones that are most important and profound. . . . The questions that such possibilities pose are fundamental questions of morality. They concern how we

---

39. Dale Jamieson presents a meticulous and compelling discussion of the limits of economics in *Reason in an Age of Darkness*, 105–43.

40. Ibid., 143.

41. Ibid., 146.

42. Ibid.

ought to live, what kinds of societies we want, and how we should relate to nature and other forms of life. Seen from this perspective, it is not surprising that economics cannot tell us everything we want to know about how we should respond to global warming and global change. *Economics may be able to tell us how to reach our goals efficiently, but it cannot tell us what our goals should be or even whether we should be concerned to reach them efficiently.*[43]

Cost-benefit analysis can show how to achieve desired ends efficiently but is ill equipped to determine whether current goals are worth pursuing, much less what the goals ought to be. In a sense, a market-based approach outsources ethics to economics in the form of cost-benefit analysis. An adequate analysis considers not only the political and economic means by which to achieve desired ends but also asks what those ends ought to be. What *is* a good life? Will more wealth necessarily make people happier? Are wild spaces worth preserving? Do nonhuman forms of life have any value in their own right, apart from their usefulness to humans? Although each of these questions has economic and political implications, they are ultimately ethical questions and must be addressed as such. Subsequent chapters will consider various moral frameworks for redefining how humans in a post-climate-change world should view their relationship to nature.

For Further Exploration

1. Given the various models of fairness considered in this chapter, what sort of international climate action agreement would be fair and why? Is it fair or unfair that developed nations such as the United States do more to address climate change than developing nations? Why or why not?

2. Conduct further research on the two primary economic ways of internalizing climate-related externalities: a carbon tax and a

---

43. Ibid., 147, emphasis added.

cap and trade program. If you were in a position to implement one of these models by fiat, which would you chose and why?

3. Can all meaningful values (e.g., the life of a human being or the existence of a species) be adequately measured economically? Why or why not?

Additional Resources

Cafaro, Philip. "Taming Growth and Articulating a Sustainable Future: The Way Forward for Environmental Ethics." *Ethics & the Environment* 16, no. 1 (2011): 1–23.

This item and the next two discuss how one might reconceive of an economy built on something other than growth and consumption.

Daly, Herman. *Ecological Economics and Sustainable Development: Selected Essays of Herman Daly.* Cheltenham, UK: Edward Elgar, 2007.

Daly, Herman E., and John Cobb Jr. *For The Common Good: Redirecting the Economy toward Community, the Environment, and a Sustainable Future.* 2nd ed. Boston: Beacon Press, 1994.

Hargrove, Eugene. "The Historical Foundations of American Environmental Attitudes." *Environmental Ethics* 1 (1979): 209–40.

A discussion of the origins of American attitudes regarding the environment.

Jamieson, Dale. "Ethics, Public Policy, and Global Warming." In *Climate Ethics: Essential Readings*, ed. Stephen M. Gardiner, Simon Caney, Dale Jamieson, and Henry Shue, 77–86. Oxford: Oxford University Press, 2010.

A comprehensive discussion of the failure of international climate change mitigation efforts.

———. *Reason in a Dark Time: Why the Struggle against Climate Change Failed—And What It Means for Our Future.* Oxford: Oxford University Press, 2014.

A comprehensive discussion of the failure of international climate change mitigation efforts. A meticulous discussion of the limits of economics in general and of William Nordhaus and Nicholas Stern in particular.

McKibben, Bill. *Deep Economy: The Wealth of Communities and the Durable Future.* New York: Times Books, 2010.

A discussion of "an economy that creates community and ennobles our lives" and is not just built on growth and consumption.

Nordhaus, William, David Popp, Zili Yang, Joseph Boyer, et al. RICE and DICE Models of Economics of Climate Change. *www.econ.yale.edu/~nordhaus/homepage/dicemodels.htm.*

Yale University economist Nordhaus and colleagues have developed two sophisticated (but ethically controversial) economic models of climate change.

Ruth, Matthias, Dana Coelho, and Daria Karetnikov. *The US Economic Impacts of Climate Change and the Costs of Inaction.* College Park: University of Maryland, 2007. *http://bit.ly/ScplH7.*

A discussion of some of the likely economic impacts of climate change.

Singer, Peter. "One Atmosphere." In *One World: The Ethics of Globalization,* 14–50. New Haven, CT: Yale University Press, 2002.

A discussion of ethics, fairness, economics, and international efforts to mitigate climate change.

Stern, Nicholas. *The Economics of Climate Change: The Stern Review.* Cambridge: Cambridge University Press, 2007.

One of the most widely cited economic analyses of climate change.

The Sustainability Paradigm

Although international and domestic political efforts to address climate change have progressed slowly, being "green" has moved from the fringes of society to become a mainstream movement. The term most closely associated with this new movement is *sustainability*. This chapter delves into the concept of sustainability and evaluates whether it provides an adequate moral framework for realizing what matters (what has value) and how humans ought to relate to the natural world.

What Is Ethics?

Anything approaching a complete introduction to ethics is beyond the scope of this volume, but it will be helpful to sketch some of its key elements.[1] Though philosophers disagree on its precise definition, *ethics* is often defined as that part of philosophy that considers questions such as "How ought I to live?," "What is the good life?," and "What has value?" To answer these questions, philosophers develop moral frameworks or theories that attempt to systematically define what the aim of life is and what has ultimate value. For instance, utilitarianism is a moral theory that argues an action is right to the extent that it brings about the greatest quantity and quality of

---

1. For a helpful introduction to ethics, consult Mark Timmons, "Introduction to Moral Theory: The Nature and Evaluation of Moral Theories," in *Conduct and Character: Readings in Moral Theory*, 6th ed. (Boston: Wadsworth, 2012), 1–16.

happiness or utility.[2] On the other hand, the moral theory of deontology argues that the aim of a moral life is not to maximize happiness but to treat rational beings with dignity and respect, as an end in themselves, never merely as a means to one's own ends.[3] In contrast to both of these views, virtue ethics is less concerned with rules for right conduct and more concerned with the moral character (virtues) required for genuine human flourishing.

Environmental ethics often expands these classical discussions to include the question of whether and when humans have moral obligations to nonhumans. Each moral framework defines the **scope of direct moral consideration**—those beings that deserve moral consideration for their own sake—based on how the theory conceives of intrinsic value or determines what things are valuable in their own right. For instance, deontology limits the scope of direct moral consideration to rational beings. In this sense, deontology is **anthropocentric**. On the other hand, because utilitarians deem pleasure intrinsically valuable, their view of morality concerns not only humans but all sentient beings, that is beings that can feel pain and pleasure. Thus utilitarianism might be seen as a sentiocentric moral framework; it limits meaning and value to sentient beings. (See sidebar "Theories of Value" for more on this.) Thus ethical theories attempt to give a systematic account of what is intrinsically valuable to provide a moral framework for how one ought to live and act. It is in this sense that ethics is concerned with attempting to define the "good life."

The challenge of anthropogenic climate change puts this classical debate in a new light. Indeed, according to the climate ethicist Dale Jamieson, current ethical systems are "inadequate and inappropriate for guiding one's thinking about global environmental problems, such as those entailed by climate changes caused by human activity."[4] According to Jamieson, a key problem with classical moral theories—such as utilitarianism, deontology, and virtue ethics—is that they

---

2. This is a particular version of utilitarianism defended by John Stuart Mill, *Utilitarianism, On Liberty, Essay on Bentham: Together with Selected Writings of Jeremy Bentham and John Austin*, ed. Mary Warnock (New York: Meridian Books, 1962).

3. This is a particular version of deontology defended by Immanuel Kant, *Grounding for the Metaphysics of Morals*, trans. James W. Ellington (Indianapolis: Hackett, 1981).

4. Dale Jamieson, "Ethics, Public Policy, and Global Warming," in *Climate Ethics: Essential Readings*, ed. Stephen M. Gardiner et al. (Oxford: Oxford University Press, 2010), 148.

were developed within the context of "low-population-density and low-technology societies, with seemingly unlimited access to land and other resources."[5] The complicated world of the twenty-first century, with its high-population-density and high-technology societies, needs to develop new moral frameworks for understanding what has value and for prescribing how humans ought to relate to the natural world.[6] Arguably, the sustainability paradigm offers one such ethical model.

Theories of Value

Axiology is the branch of philosophy that concerns the definition and scope of value. Axiological theories of value define the scope of direct moral concern for each ethical framework, or those beings that are deserving of **direct moral duties** for their own sake. Within environmental ethics, much of axiology focuses on defining what a being has to be like in order to have not merely **instrumental value** based on its usefulness but also **intrinsic value** for its own sake.

- *Anthropocentrism*: All and only human beings have intrinsic value and deserve to be morally considered for their own sake. All non-humans have merely instrumental value and do not deserve direct moral consideration.[7]

- *Sentiocentrism*: All beings with the ability to feel pleasure and pain have intrinsic value and deserve to be morally

Continued

---

5. Ibid.

6. For a more extensive discussion of the unique features of global climate change that present a challenge to traditional moral theories, see Stephen M. Gardiner, "A Perfect Moral Storm: Climate Change, Intergenerational Ethics, and the Problem of Corruption," in *Climate Ethics: Essential Readings*, ed. Stephen M. Gardiner et al. (Oxford: Oxford University Press, 2010), 87–98. Gardiner has developed this position into a monograph: Stephen M. Gardiner, *A Perfect Moral Storm: The Ethical Tragedy of Climate Change* (Oxford: Oxford University Press, 2011).

7. Immanuel Kant is representative of an anthropocentric axiology. In his *Lectures on Ethics*, he writes, "But so far as animals are concerned, we have no direct duties. Animals are not self-conscious and are there merely as a means to an end. That end is man." Trans. Louis Infield (London: Methuen, 1930), 239.

Theories of Value *Continued*

considered for their own sake. All non-sentient beings have merely instrumental value and do not deserve direct moral consideration.[8]

- *Biocentrism:* All living beings have intrinsic value and deserve to be morally considered for their own sake. All non-living beings have merely instrumental value and do not deserve direct moral consideration.[9]

- *Ecocentrism:* All living beings as well as the systems of which they are a part have intrinsic value and deserve to be morally considered for their own sake. Since everything on Earth, living or non-living, is part of a system of living beings, nothing is excluded from the scope of direct moral consideration for ecocentrism. All living and non-living things deserve direct moral consideration.[10]

---

8. Peter Singer is representative of a sentiocentric axiology. He argues that "the capacity for suffering and enjoyment is a *prerequisite for having interests at all,* a condition that must be satisfied before we can speak of interests in a meaningful way. . . . The capacity for suffering and enjoyment is, however, not only necessary, but also sufficient for us to say that a being has interests—at an absolute minimum, an interest in not suffering." *Animal Liberation,* updated ed. (New York: Harper Perennial, [1975] 2009), 8–9, emphasis added.

9. Robin Attfield defends what he calls "biocentric consequentialism." He defines biocentrism as "a stance that holds that all living creatures have a good of their own, and have moral standing accordingly, and that their flourishing or attaining their good is intrinsically valuable." *Environmental Ethics* (Oxford: Polity, 2003), 189. Gary Varner notes that views such as this are a form of what he calls "biocentric individualism," in that they "attribute moral standing to all living things while denying that holistic entities like species or ecosystems have moral standing." "Biocentric Individualism," in *Environmental Ethics: Divergence and Convergence,* 3rd ed., ed. Susan J. Armstrong and Richard G. Botzler (New York: McGrawHill, 2004), 357.

10. Unlike the other axiological theories, ecocentrism is holistic rather than individualistic; it affirms the value of not only individual living beings but also ecosystems. One version of ecocentrism defended by Bill Devall and George Sessions is called "deep ecology." Deep ecology holds that "all things in the biosphere have an equal right to live and blossom and to reach their own individual forms of unfolding and self-realization within the larger Self-realization. This basic intuition is that all organisms and entities in the ecosphere, as parts of the interrelated whole, are equal in intrinsic worth." *Deep Ecology: Living as If Nature Mattered* (Salt Lake City: Gibbs Smith, 1985), 67.

The Rise of the Sustainability Paradigm

Within both government and the popular media, the concept of "sustainability" has become the most common way of referring to the needed shift in attitudes and practices in order to address the challenge of global climate change.[11] As the influential environmental philosopher Bryan Norton puts it,

> In our search for an environmental ethic we will never . . . find any environmental values or goals more defensible than the sustainability principle, which asserts that each generation has an obligation to protect productive ecological and physical processes necessary to support options necessary for future human freedom and welfare.[12]

Sustainability is, he asserts, the "keystone concept of modern environmentalism."[13]

The term *sustainability* does not have particularly deep historical roots. According to one study, the word *sustainable* was originally used by the military to mean "capable of being defended," implying the need for defense against aggression and suggesting a future orientation. Implicitly, it also recognizes limits beyond which defense would not be possible.[14] In the mid-nineteenth century the term had a juridical meaning of "capable of being upheld or defended as valid, correct, or true."[15] In the 1960s, economists started to use the

---

11. Portions of this section on sustainability appear in Brian G. Henning, "Sustainability and Other Ecological Mistakes," in *Beyond Superlatives*, ed. Roland Faber, J. R. Hustwit, and Hollis Phelps (Newcastle upon Tyne: Cambridge Scholars Press, 2014), 76–89. Published with permission of Cambridge Scholars Publishing.

12. Bryan G. Norton, "Integration or Reduction: Two Approaches to Environmental Values," in *Environmental Pragmatism*, ed. Andrew Light and Eric Katz (New York: Routledge, 1996), 122.

13. Ibid. It is important to note that Norton himself defines *sustainability* more broadly than the UN Brundtland Commission. My use of his work here is to establish the centrality of the concept, not to present the author as a proponent of the mainstream definition. For more on Norton's view, see Bryan G. Norton, *Searching for Sustainability: Interdisciplinary Essays in the Philosophy of Conservation Biology* (Cambridge: Cambridge University Press, 2003).

14. Daniel J. Sherman, "Sustainability: What's the Big Idea? A Strategy for Transforming the Higher Education Curriculum," *Sustainability* 1, no. 3 (2008): 192.

15. "Sustainability, n.," OED Online, March 2014, Oxford University Press, *http://bit.ly/1hvbty8*.

term *sustainable growth* to mean the use of resources that is capable of being maintained at a certain rate or level. In this sense, *sustainability* actually means maximum sustainable extraction, or the highest rate of extraction consistent with ecosystem maintenance. Thus "sustainable fishing" would be the largest possible catch consistent with maintaining the stock's capacity for self-renewal.[16] Though the term as used today refers to more than questions of mere resource extraction, it nevertheless bears the marks of its practical birth.

According to David Orr, professor of environmental studies and politics at Oberlin College and a leader of the modern sustainability movement, the concept of sustainability entered the public discourse in the late 1970s and early 1980s with the work of scholars such as Wes Jackson and Lester Brown.[17] The concept gained international prominence in 1987, when the United Nations' Brundtland Commission argued that sustainable development should "become a central guiding principle of the United Nations, governments and private institutions, organizations and enterprises."[18] Notably, the commission defined sustainable development as "meeting the needs of the present without compromising the ability of future generations to meet their own needs."[19] Despite subsequent formulations and elaborations, this concise version remains for many the central definition of the sustainability paradigm.

Key to this notion of sustainability is the recognition that human society and human economy does not take place in a vacuum, but within a natural context, and that context has biophysical limits. People now know that most natural resources are not unlimited and that they must take care that these resources remain available not only for the present generation but also for future generations. Thus for many, the sustainability paradigm is primarily concerned with transitioning from carbon-intensive forms of energy production and transportation (such as coal and oil) to greener forms of energy production (such as solar, geothermal, and wind) and transportation (such as electric

16. Norton, "Integration or Reduction," 97.

17. David Orr, "Four Challenges of Sustainability," *Conservation Biology* 16, no. 6 (December 2002): 1457.

18. United Nations General Assembly, 96th Plenary Meeting, *Report of the World Commission on Environment and Development*, A/RES/42/187, December 11, 1987.

19. Ibid.

cars and high-speed trains). In this way, the sustainability paradigm focuses mostly on creating more efficient, less polluting forms of technology. It attempts to expand humanity's focus on short-term profits and narrow concern for the present to the impact of various forms of living on future generations. It asks humans to consider how they can achieve their ends today without compromising the ability of future generations to satisfy their own needs.

Sustainability on Campus

College campuses have been at the forefront of sustainability initiatives. In the United States, many institutions of higher education have effectively modeled strategies for addressing climate change, with the American College & University Presidents' Climate Commitment (ACUPCC) being a prime example. Since its launch in 2007, more than 680 institutions have become signatories.[20] The following is a selection from the Commitment:

> We, the undersigned presidents and chancellors of colleges and universities, are deeply concerned about the unprecedented scale and speed of global warming and its potential for large-scale, adverse health, social, economic and ecological effects. We recognize the scientific consensus that global warming is real and is largely being caused by humans. . . .
>
> We believe colleges and universities must exercise leadership in their communities and throughout society by modeling ways to minimize global warming emissions, and by providing the knowledge and the educated graduates to achieve climate neutrality. Campuses that address the climate challenge by reducing global warming emissions and by integrating sustainability into their curriculum will better serve their students and meet their social mandate to help create a thriving, ethical and civil society. . . .
>
> We further believe that colleges and universities that exert leadership in addressing climate change will stabilize

Continued

20. American College & University Presidents' Climate Commitment, last modified 2014, *www.presidentsclimatecommitment.org.*

Sustainability on Campus *Continued*

and reduce their long-term energy costs, attract excellent students and faculty, attract new sources of funding, and increase the support of alumni and local communities.[21]

In becoming a signatory, every institution commits, among other things, to (1) inventory and publicly report on a biennial basis its greenhouse gas emissions, (2) create a climate action plan outlining when and how the institution plans to reduce its carbon footprint, and (3) design ways to incorporate sustainability themes and principles into its research and curriculum. The ultimate goal is to achieve **carbon neutrality**—having no net greenhouse gas emissions.[22] Though a relatively new effort, real results have begun to materialize. As of 2013, 471 institutions had submitted more than one GHG inventory, reflecting a cumulative *annual* reduction of carbon dioxide equivalent (CO_2e) by 328,698 metric tons. Further, 240 of these institutions have shown a reduction totaling 2,094,395 metric tons.[23] Part of these reductions have come through the transition to renewable energy. Collectively, signatories of the Climate Commitment annually produce 444,300,134 kilowatt hours. This is the equivalent of powering 46,928 American households annually.[24]

---

21. "Text of the American College & University Presidents' Climate Commitment," American College & University Presidents' Climate Commitment, last modified 2013, *http://bit.ly/1lPmhs2*.

22. "For purposes of the ACUPCC, climate neutrality is defined as having no net GHG emissions, to be achieved by minimizing GHG emissions as much as possible, and using carbon offsets or other measures to mitigate the remaining emissions if necessary. . . . The concept of 'carbon neutrality,' 'climate neutrality,' or 'GHG neutrality' has been evolving and there is currently no universally agreed-upon definition of the term. Signatories should be aware that these terms are often used interchangeably, and for the purposes of the ACUPCC the above definition is used for all three terms." "The ACUPCC Voluntary Carbon Offset Protocol," American College & University Presidents' Climate Commitment, *http://bit.ly/1kcoGvC*. Gonzaga University, for example, became a signatory to the ACUPCC in January 2011 and completed its climate action plan in January 2013. It has pledged to reduce its greenhouse gas emissions by 20% by 2020 and 50% by 2035, with the goal of becoming carbon neutral by 2050. See *www.gonzaga.edu/ClimateActionPlan*.

23. "ACUPCC Progress Summary," American College & University Presidents' Climate Commitment, June 2013, *http://bit.ly/TR7aZ3*.

24. Ibid.

Beyond Sustainability

In many ways, the concept of sustainability is vitally important. Humanity desperately needs to change its practices if it is to sustain a climate in which it can thrive. Moreover, as it is defined by the United Nations within international law, the concept of sustainability is valuable because it helps to introduce an intergenerational focus. The concept of sustainability moves people past the myopia of the present, requiring that in meeting its needs the present generation should not comprise the ability of future generations to meet theirs. Despite its importance, however, some observers question whether the sustainability paradigm ultimately provides an adequate moral framework for confronting climate change because of its (1) anthropocentrism, (2) heavy reliance on technology, and (3) lack of determinate moral content.

Sustainability as Anthropocentric

First, as most commonly used, the concept of sustainability limits intrinsic value to present and future humans; in other words, it is anthropocentric. Taken literally, *anthropocentrism* simply means human-centered (see sidebar "Theories of Value"). In one sense, all thought is unavoidably anthropocentric in that it takes place from the perspective of human experience. Similarly, because humans are complex enough to be conscious and free enough to be responsible, one might accurately characterize all discussions of ethics, indeed all branches of investigation, as unavoidably anthropocentric.[25] However, in the context of ethics, holding an anthropocentric worldview goes beyond this basic orientation and concludes that *the natural world only has meaning and value insofar as it is related to humans.* It is this further assumption—that nothing has value apart from its relationship to humans—that has been used to excuse and perpetuate a destructive attitude toward the natural world. Is this anthropocentric attitude justified?

---

25. The criteria of "complex enough to be conscious and free enough to be responsible" are intentionally vague and establish empirical conditions that need to be met to be considered a moral agent. Whether healthy adult humans are the only moral agents is still an open question. Other beings may in fact meet these conditions and would therefore be moral agents.

With the publishing of *The Descent of Man, and Selection in Relation to Sex* (1871), Charles Darwin fundamentally challenged how people view their place in the cosmic order.[26] Humanity was no longer categorically set at the pinnacle of, or apart from, nature (although people historically have been reluctant to give up their anthropocentrism, even while intellectually assenting to an evolutionary worldview).[27] For millennia, philosophers and theologians had depicted humans as utterly unique, but Darwin revealed this as a great delusion; humans had been viewing nature from a self-constructed pedestal. According to Darwin, evolutionary change occurs gradually. Therefore, if humans have emotions, language, and a highly developed capacity for reason and culture-making, among other traits, then their evolutionary ancestors must also have had similar, though perhaps less acute, capacities. Evolutionary theory requires the abandonment of simplistic, binary conceptions. Language, reason, emotion, and culture are not all-or-nothing categories; rather, many living creatures possess these traits to varying degrees.

In his book *Next of Kin*, Roger Fouts provides powerful evidence for the claim that other creatures possess "human" characteristics. While working his way through graduate school, Fouts took a job as a lab assistant for two psychologists who were exploring whether it was possible to teach a chimpanzee named Washoe a human language, American Sign Language (ASL) (see fig. 4.1). This unintentional encounter started what would become a lifelong relationship between Washoe and Fouts. Washoe learned, not by memorizing and mimicking, but by participating in a language community.[28] Washoe could understand hundreds of signs and combine them to communicate in syntactically correct sentences.

---

26. The following six paragraphs have been adapted from Brian G. Henning, "From Exception to Exemplification: Understanding the Debate over Darwin," in *Genesis, Evolution, and the Search for a Reasoned Faith*, ed. Mary Kate Birge et al. (Winona, MN: Anselm Academic, 2011), 73–98.

27. *Anthropocentrism* literally means "human-centered." It is the view that all meaning and value is derived from an entity's relationship to humans; an entity has no value outside its relationship to humans. See sidebar titled "Theories of Value" on page 98.

28. Roger Fouts and Stephen Tukel Mills, *Next of Kin: My Conversations with Chimpanzees* (New York: Avon Books, 1997), 77–90.

Her performance, at four years of age, was remarkable. She scored 86 percent correct in one representative test that had 64 trials, and on a test twice as long—128 trials—she scored 71 percent. (Guessing randomly on this test would produce a score of 4 percent.) . . . [A]t age five, Washoe was using 132 signs reliably and could understand hundreds of others. In addition to naming and categorizing objects, Washoe began doing something that [Noam] Chomsky said only humans could do: she assembled words into novel combinations.[29]

Perhaps even more striking, in a later stage of the experiment, without any influence from the human staff, Washoe taught ASL to her adopted son, Loulis. Fouts shows in story after story how Washoe made jokes, could understand some complex concepts, planned for the future, and nearly died from a severe depression caused by the death of her newborn son.[30] He observes, "The apparently intelligent chimpanzee now threatened to bring down the entire artifice of Aristotle's Great Chain of Being."[31]

© www.friendsofwashoe.org; Friends of Washoe, Ellensburg, WA

Fouts's point was not that there was no difference between himself and Washoe or between humans and chimpanzees. Important differences in the abilities of chimps and humans exist, but these

Figure 4.1. Washoe, a chimpanzee, was the first non-human to learn a human language (ASL) and pass it on to offspring.

---

29. Ibid., 100–101.

30. Researchers intervened and introduced Washoe to the ten-month-old male chimpanzee, Loulis, whom she adopted as her own. Washoe died at the age of 42 in 2007.

31. Fouts and Mills, *Next of Kin*, 50.

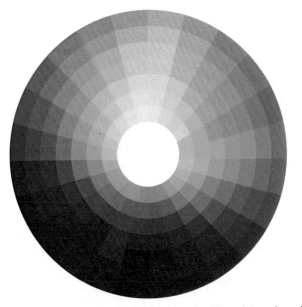

© ekler/Shutterstock.com

Figure 4.2. Difference of degree and kind can be likened to colors. Slight changes in the intensity (degree) of a color can accumulate to result in completely different colors (kind).

differences are ultimately a matter of degree, not kind. To be more precise, differences of kind are a consequence of differences of degree.

To understand this claim regarding differences, imagine the colors red, orange, and yellow on the color spectrum. While red, orange, and yellow are each a different *kind* of color, the differences between these distinct colors are ultimately a result of differences of *degree*. Minute changes in the intensity of the color red gradually shift to become orange, which gradually becomes yellow, and so on (see fig. 4.2). Notice that between these colors it is impossible to select one particular point and say, "Here, this is clearly only red and not orange," or "This is clearly only orange and not yellow." Rather, there is orange-yellow and then yellow-orange and so on.[32] There is no clear demarcation. However, this does not deny that red, orange, and

---

32. Crayon manufacturers are creative in picking names to reflect these subtle color changes, referring to *yellow*, as well as *daisy yellow*, *goldenrod*, and *sunset*.

yellow are distinctly different colors. When differences of degree accumulate sufficiently, they result in differences of kind.

In the same way, evolutionary theory teaches that each species is a product of gradual accumulations of minute changes over millions of years—changes that result in distinct species of animals, such as chimps and humans. Chimps are clearly one kind of animal and humans another, but the differences between them are ultimately only a matter of degree. In an important way, this is what the experiment with Washoe demonstrates. If chimpanzees are indeed humanity's closest evolutionary relatives, sharing 99.4% of our DNA,[33] then, Fouts reasoned, they ought to be capable of complex thought and language.

This is exactly what he found. Properly understood, the theory of evolution questions simplistic claims of human uniqueness, claims that humans alone are capable of consciousness, self-awareness, reason, language, and emotion. If humans have evolved over tens of millions of years from other life forms, then, of necessity, their evolutionary ancestors possess these traits in simpler forms.

Fully appreciating humanity's place within nature makes even sustainability's enlightened view problematic. The concept of sustainability does replace an arrogant, destructive anthropocentrism, one that implies humans can use nature with impunity, with a more enlightened anthropocentrism that focuses both on present and future humans. However, when sustainability serves as *the* framing moral category, ultimately all value and meaning emanates from and depends on humanity; nothing has value apart from its relationship to humans.

Given the age and size of the universe and humanity's relatively recent appearance, such a position betrays a certain hubris. As discussed in chapter 1, the universe is some 13.75 billion years old. Earth itself has existed for 4.5 billion years of that span, with *Homo sapiens* being a relative latecomer, appearing only 200,000 years ago.[34] A thoroughgoing anthropocentrism entails the belief

---

33. "Having branched off from humans more recently (perhaps 5.4 million years ago), chimps are genetically more similar to humans (0.6 percent difference in DNA) than to gorillas (2.3 percent difference) or orangutans (3.6 percent difference)." Fouts and Mills, *Next of Kin*, 55.

34. See volumes diagram (fig. 1.4) in chapter 1.

that the millions of creatures existing prior to the evolution of humans had no value because there were no humans to value them.[35] The dimensions of the social and ecological crises humanity faces in the twenty-first century calls for a rejection of all forms of anthropocentrism.

Sustainability and Technophilia (Love of Technology)

A second critique of the sustainability paradigm charges that it is too often grounded in an uncritical **technophilia** or love of technology. For a time, biologists even defined humans in terms of their engineering prowess—referring to them as *Homo faber*, man the maker—until Jane Goodall observed chimpanzees making rudimentary tools. For decades, literature and popular media have attempted to conceive of the bright and shiny technological utopia that awaits society in the future.

For instance, the cartoon classic *The Jetsons*, which first aired in the 1960s, depicts everything that mid-twentieth-century America wanted—flying cars, robot maids, moving sidewalks, and jet packs! Many such innovations have in fact come into existence, including moving sidewalks (e.g., in airports) and vacuuming robots (e.g., Roomba). Though flying cars and jet packs remain absent, humanity's technophilia seems to know no bounds. For thousands of years humans have successfully used technology to overcome physical limitations. In one of the more remarkable feats, NASA recently landed a car-size, laser-toting, plutonium-powered robot on the surface of Mars.

Perhaps, though, the future *The Jetsons* envisioned is as much a depiction of an environmental **dystopia** as a technological utopia. The cartoon depicts a world utterly devoid of nature. Indeed, human civilization does not even live on the surface of the planet anymore; homes, stores, schools, and factories sit on tall columns far above it.

---

35. Biologist Stephen J. Gould had a memorable, if hyperbolic, way of responding to such a view. "Nature does not exist for us, had no idea we were coming, and doesn't give a damn about us." "The Golden Rule: A Proper Scale for Our Environmental Crisis," *Natural History* 99, no. 9 (September 1990): 24.

When venturing "outside," each person is encased in a bubble, presumably because the atmosphere is too thin. While the creators of the show no doubt wanted to depict life in space, the possibility that humans will foul the planet so much as to make it impossible to live on its surface seems within reach.

Maybe *The Jetsons* should not be viewed as the model for a bright and shiny future but rather as a cautionary tale like the 2008 animated movie *WALL-E*, which depicts a planet so polluted by rampant consumerism that humans have had to abandon it. In that film, humans live far from Earth in a giant spaceship, where robots wait on them hand and foot. Obese people float around on hovering chairs, drinking all of their calories in liquid form and only interacting with the humans around them through screens. Though fictional, *The Jetsons* and *WALL-E* present one possible outcome of a complete and uncritical reliance on technology.

Engineers often ask "how" questions: How can we put a rover on Mars? How can we create cleaner forms of energy production and transportation? Economists then talk about achieving those aims efficiently. The "should" questions, however, often remain unasked. These are the questions that ethics must consider. It is

Figure 4.3. In 2012, in one of the greatest engineering feats, US scientists used a supersonic parachute and a "sky crane" to safely land a car-sized robotic rover (aptly named "Curiosity") on the planet Mars, 33.9 million miles from Earth.

one thing to ask, "Can we survive in a post-climate-change world?" or "Can Earth support 12 billion people?" It is quite another to ask, "Should we *aspire* to live in a world devoid of nature?" Neither engineering nor economics can advise humanity on what its aims should be or whether it should concern itself with achieving them efficiently.[36] Only one's values, one's ethics, can answer these questions. Even if technology *could* create a *Jetsons*-like future, *should* it? Do humans want to live in a stainless steel world where nature is completely absent?

The second concern with the sustainability paradigm, then, is that it potentially reduces a fundamentally moral issue concerning how humanity ought to live to a technical issue in need of "management." As Jamieson argues,

> Management approaches are doomed to failure . . . [because] the questions they can answer are not the ones that are most important and profound. . . . The questions that such possibilities [such as climate change] pose are fundamental questions of morality. They concern how we ought to live, what kinds of societies we want, and how we should relate to nature and other forms of life.[37]

Critics contend that the sustainability paradigm encourages the reduction of morality to a social scientific analysis of economic values achievable through technological innovation. It outsources morality to economics and engineering. They argue that developing and deploying cleaner forms of technology, while certainly needed, is not enough. Humans also need to rethink who they are and how they relate to the natural world, to re-envision how they conceive of a good life well lived.

Sustainability as Morally Neutral

The third and perhaps most significant shortcoming of using sustainability as the fundamental moral category to define the relationship between humans and nature is the almost complete absence of

---

36. Jamieson, "Ethics, Public Policy, and Global Warming," 147.

37. Ibid., 146–47.

moral content.[38] The concept of sustainability does not ask, much less answer, fundamental questions of value such as, "Is the modern consumer society, even if it could be made sustainable, truly a good life?" The paradigm suggests pursuing sustainable policies but does not identify which policies are, in fact, worth sustaining. One could be *sustained* within a concentration camp, but no one would welcome such conditions. In terms of climate change, would it be morally acceptable to leave future inhabitants of the planet in the natural equivalent of a concentration camp? The sustainability paradigm does not clearly rule out these possibilities. Indeed, one can make such justifications and judgments only when the framework incorporates more basic value commitments.

Although important, in the end, the mainstream form of the sustainability paradigm is more a biological principle than an ethical principle. It does not function well as an ethical concept because it is divorced from more fundamental moral discussions of the "good life," of value. The problem is that morally deficient activities can be made ecologically sustainable: the prisoner in the concentration camp and the hen in the battery cage can be sustained. Sustainability offers no insight into what ends are worth sustaining. By presupposing rather than engaging in debate over the goals humanity should pursue, the mainstream sustainability paradigm creates a theoretical void that the status quo is more than happy to fill. "We're so used to *growth* that we can't imagine alternatives," writes McKibben, "[and] at best we embrace the squishy *sustainable*, with its implied claim that we can keep on as before."[39] Without explicit discussions of the nature of the good, what is inevitably sustained is the status quo and its thin conceptions of the "good life." It reduces ethics to mere survival.

---

38. Despite the lack of moral content in the sustainability paradigm, the view that sustainability is a moral or normative concept is common. For example, the Rock Ethics Institute at Pennsylvania State University argues that "sustainability is a normative concept. Sustainability is considered to be positive and is used as a guiding principle for individual and political actions. An adequate recognition and analysis of the ethical meaning of the concept of sustainability is necessary in order to generate encompassing and adequate analyses and solutions of sustainability issues." "Sustainability Ethics," *http://rockethics.psu.edu/climate/sustainability-ethics*.

39. Bill McKibben, *Eaarth: Making a Life on a Tough New Planet* (New York: Time Books, 2010), 102–3.

Developing an Environmental Ethic

In sum, then, the mainstream sustainability paradigm proves inadequate because it is anthropocentric (in that it limits all value to humans), uncritically technophilic (in that it reduces ethics to a form of resource management), and empty of any particular moral content. The sustainability paradigm's lack of moral content and its neutrality regarding what kind of life should be sustained makes it unsuitable to serve as the primary moral category for an adequate environmental ethic.

Although debates over carbon taxes, trading schemes, hybrid cars, and compact fluorescent light bulbs are important, efforts to address climate change will ultimately fail unless and until humanity sets about the difficult work of reconceiving itself and how it relates to the environment. Humans need new ways of thinking and acting that recognize their fundamental interdependence and interconnection with everyone and everything in the cosmos—ways of understanding that recognize the intrinsic beauty and value of every form of existence. To capture the fact that the concept of sustainability does bring to the moral discussion some important tools, perhaps it would be helpful to distinguish between a "shallow" notion of sustainability, which limits its concern to present and future humans, and a "deep" notion of sustainability that seeks to include the entire biotic community. Redefined and set within a larger moral framework to address the situation of climate change, perhaps a more robust notion of sustainability can be a helpful moral concept. The next chapter will consider whether the concept of ecological stewardship provides that larger moral framework that could serve as a more adequate basis for conceiving of our moral relationship to the biotic community.

For Further Exploration

1. Is your school a signatory of the American College & University Presidents' Climate Commitment? Check their website (*http://bit.ly/1kcsgWq*). If so, what are the stated emission reductions and time line for your institution?

2. Princeton University's Carbon Mitigation Initiative (*http://cmi.princeton.edu/wedges/*) has developed an activity called the Stabilization Wedges Game that nicely illustrates a technological approach to sustainability. On the website the materials for the game can be downloaded, including a useful teacher guide. The Stabilization Wedges Game is a team-based exercise that teaches players about the scale of the greenhouse gas problem, plus technologies that already exist to dramatically reduce our carbon emissions. Players pick eight carbon-cutting strategies to construct a carbon mitigation portfolio, filling in the eight wedges of the stabilization triangle. It makes a great in-class activity or something to explore on one's own.

3. Calculate and reflect on your own "ecological footprint" and that of your family. Based on this research, you can consider selecting practices to experimentally modify.

> *Step 1*: Estimate your footprint (the amount of land area required to sustain your use of natural resources). Could everyone on the planet live like you do? Record your views.
>
> *Step 2*: Research what a sustainable level of per capita CO_2e emissions would be. In other words, approximately how many tons of CO_2e could each person emit annually to keep CO_2 at or below 350 ppm? Explain how you arrived at your calculation.
>
> *Step 3*: Calculate your *personal* "ecological footprint" by completing at least two of the following ecological footprint quizzes. Record your findings in a separate document. Review the footprint quiz website to determine how the footprint is calculated and record your findings.
>
> - Redefining Progess, Ecological Footprint: *www.ecologicalfootprint.org/*
> - Environmental Protection Agency (EPA) Individual Greenhouse Gas Emissions Calculator: *http://1.usa.gov/1kcpdh7*
> - Earth Day Network Footprint Calculator: *http://bit.ly/1lf68Rg*
> - The Nature Conservancy, "What's My Carbon Footprint": *http://bit.ly/1cXA1QX*

Step 4: Calculate your family's (or roommates') "carbon footprint." Visit the EPA's Household Carbon Footprint Calculator (*http://1.usa.gov/1dKe1ao*) and make a list of the information that you will have to collect (e.g., average electrical bill for your home). (You might also do the household calculator at the Nature Conservancy mentioned above.) After collecting the necessary information, use the online calculator to obtain an estimate of your family's greenhouse gas emissions. Record your findings. Visit the EPA's "What You Can Do" webpage (including the section on dorm life) to explore actions you and your family can take to lower your emissions while reducing your energy and waste disposal costs. Record your findings and discussion. If your family is already doing the suggestions listed by the EPA, do a little bit of research to find ten ways to reduce your carbon footprint.

Step 5: In light of what you've learned, what if anything would you change about your habits? Record your thoughts. Write an essay that critically examines your own habits and the habits of your family. Try to identify one to three practices that you and/or your family are willing to change, at least on an experimental basis.

Additional Resources

ORGANIZATIONS

American College & University Presidents' Climate Commitment, *www.presidentsclimatecommitment.org*

> The website includes a summary of the progress achieved through the Climate Commitment so far, "ACUPCC Progress Summary," June 2013, *http://bit.ly/TR7aZ3*.

Association for the Advancement of Sustainability in Higher Education, *www.aashe.org*

> Resources on sustainability in higher education.

Rock Ethics Institute, Pennsylvania State University, *http://rockethics*
.psu.edu/

> A wealth of resources related to ethics, climate change, and sustainability, including

> - Ethics in Climate Change, *http://rockethics.psu.edu/climate/*
> - Ethical Dimensions of Climate Change, *http://rockethics*
>   *.psu.edu/climate/edcc*
> - The Gender Justice and Global Climate Change Network,
>   *http://rockethics.psu.edu/climate/g2c2*
> - Sustainability Ethics, *http://rockethics.psu.edu/climate*
>   */sustainability-ethics*

Sustainability Research Institute, University of Leeds, UK, *www.see*
.leeds.ac.uk/research/sri/

> Conducts "internationally recognised, academically excellent and problem-oriented interdisciplinary research and teaching on environmental, social and economic aspects of sustainability."

BOOKS AND ARTICLES

Gardiner, Stephen M., Simon Caney, Dale Jamieson, and Henry
Shue, eds. *Climate Ethics: Essential Readings*. New York: Oxford,
2010.

> A diverse (but not comprehensive) anthology on climate ethics.

Writings by Stephen M. Gardiner, Department of Philosophy,
University of Washington, *www.phil.washington.edu/users*
/gardiner-stephen

> Gardiner is a leading ethicist discussing climate change. His writings include

> - "Ethics and Global Climate Change." *Ethics* 114 (April
>   2004): 555–600.
>
>   An excellent article summarizing the key ethical issues involved in anthropogenic climate change.
>
> - "A Perfect Moral Storm: Climate Change, Intergenerational Ethics, and the Problem of Corruption." *Environmental Values* 15 (2006): 397–413.

- *A Perfect Moral Storm: The Ethical Tragedy of Climate Change.* New York: Oxford University Press, 2011.

  Extensive discussions of the unique features of global climate change that present a challenge to traditional moral theories.

Writings by Dale Jamieson, Environmental Studies, New York University, *http://environment.as.nyu.edu/object/dalejamieson.html*

Jamieson is a leading ethicist discussing climate change. See especially his

- "Ethics, Public Policy, and Global Warming." In *Climate Ethics: Essential Readings*, ed. Stephen M. Gardiner, Simon Caney, Dale Jamieson, and Henry Shue, 77–85. New York: Oxford University Press, 2010.

- *Reason in a Dark Time: Why the Struggle against Climate Change Failed—And What It Means for Our Future.* New York: Oxford University Press, 2014.

Norton, Bryan G. "Integration or Reduction: Two Approaches to Environmental Values." In *Environmental Pragmatism*, ed. Andrew Light and Eric Katz. New York: Routledge, 1996.

A defense of sustainability.

———. *Searching for Sustainability: Interdisciplinary Essays in the Philosophy of Conservation Biology.* Cambridge: Cambridge University Press, 2003.

Orr, David W. *Earth in Mind: On Education, Environment, and the Human Prospect.* Washington, DC: Island Press, 2004.

This and the next four sources discuss the role of the concept of sustainability within higher education.

———. *Ecological Literacy: Education and the Transition to a Postmodern World.* Albany: State University of New York Press, 1992.

———. "Four Challenges of Sustainability." *Conservation Biology* 16, no. 6 (December 2002).

Sherman, Daniel J. "Sustainability: What's the Big Idea? A Strategy for Transforming the Higher Education Curriculum." *Sustainability* 1, no. 3 (2008).

Stone, Michael K., and Zenobia Barlow, eds. *Ecological Literacy: Educating Our Children for a Sustainable World*. San Francisco: Sierra Club Books, 2005.

United Nations Brundtland Report, "Our Common Future," 1987, *http://en.wikisource.org/wiki/Brundtland_Report*.

Defines sustainability within international policy.

5

CHAPTER

Ecological Stewardship and the Great Work

The previous chapter argued that the mainstream conception of sustainability is likely insufficient by itself to describe humanity's relationship to the natural world because it too narrowly focuses on humans (it is anthropocentric), it uncritically accepts technological solutions to environmental problems (it is technophilic), and it stays morally neutral regarding value and the nature of the good life. To help move toward a deeper conception of sustainability, this chapter considers whether the concept of *ecological stewardship* offers a richer moral context for conceiving of humanity's relationship to the natural world and responding to the challenges of anthropogenic climate change.

From Despot to Steward

When introducing the concept of "stewardship" to environmental ethics students, I often appeal to the model found in the third volume of J. R. R. Tolkien's *Lord of the Rings* trilogy. In addition to being a wonderful adventure story, Tolkein's trilogy is, like so many in its genre, about the Manichean struggle between good and evil. The forces of goodness are symbolized by the green and living things in the world, represented in the stories by elves, wizards, and especially hobbits—simple beings that lead lives close to the earth. The forces of evil are symbolized by darkness, death, technological destruction, and domination of nature, represented in the stories by orcs, goblins, and trolls. The narrative arc of the three volumes is about an evil "Ring of Power" that, if it were to fall into the wrong hands, could tip the balance and allow the forces of destruction to overwhelm the world. By happenstance, the ring has come into the possession of a hobbit named Bilbo, who later bequeaths it to his adopted nephew Frodo.

The third volume of the trilogy, *The Return of the King*, describes the kingdom of Gondor. For centuries Gondor had been ruled by benevolent and wise rulers in the line of Númenor who were blessed with particularly long life. Because of the corrupting influence of the ring of power, the line of Númenor was nearly broken. There was but one person—a man named Aragorn—who had forsaken his crown and become a "Ranger of the North." Thus, the kingdom of Gondor had come to be ruled not by kings of Númenor but by stewards, who are charged with care of the kingdom until the rightful king returns. In the time of the story, Gondor is ruled by Denethor II, twenty-sixth steward of Gondor. Denethor is a proud but broken man who starts to become unhinged upon learning that his favored first son, Boramir, died while on a mission to find and return with the "Ring of Power." Shortly after learning of Boramir's death, Denethor's second son, Faramir, is apparently fatally wounded while defending the city of Minas Tirith from the evil armies of Mordor. This causes Denethor to finally lose his mind. He orders the body of his injured but very much alive son Faramir be placed on a funeral pyre and burned. If not for the last-minute intervention of the Hobbit Peregrin Took and the wizard Gandolf, Faramir would have been burned alive. In his delusional state, Denethor lights himself on fire and is consumed on the pyre he lit for his son.

This fictional example highlights essential aspects of ecological stewardship, and perhaps serves as a cautionary tale. Denethor's poor care of the kingdom of Gondor ultimately led to his self-destruction. Given the anthropogenic ecological crisis, some might say humanity is in danger of being compared to Denethor. Poor care of Earth could lead to humanity's demise. Central to the concept of stewardship is its contrast to the idea of ownership. As the Steward, Denethor does not "own" the kingdom of Gondor. The people are not *his* subjects and the land is not *his* possession to dispose of as he pleases. Rather, like stewards before him, Denethor is charged with protecting the people and lands of Gondor until the "return of the king." This conveys the idea that stewardship undermines the model of an *owner*, with rights and privileges over his subjects, and replaces it with that of a *caretaker* who is answerable to another. As an analogy for conceiving of humanity's relationship to nature, the caretaker model emphasizes that Earth and its many inhabitants do not belong to humans to be disposed of as they please. However, this model implies the question: if humans are stewards of nature, to whom or to what do they answer? We will consider several different answers to this question.

Secular Stewardship

Though not as widely known as sustainability, the concept of stewardship has popular secular appeal. Biologist Tim Flannery appeals to the model in his book *The Weather Makers,* and climate scientist John Houghton, a founding co-chair of the United Nation's Intergovernmental Panel on Climate Change (IPCC), refers to it in his definitive textbook *Global Warming: The Complete Briefing*. However, in a secular context, the question of "answerability" is not straightforward. In whose name are humans stewards? The answer to this question depends on one's axiology or one's conception of the locus and scope of value (see sidebar "Theories of Value" in chap. 4).

If one adopts an anthropocentric view, limiting all meaning and value to humans, then one is ultimately answerable only to humans. However, this need not imply a crass or narrow anthropocentrism. If one is answerable not merely to present humans but also future generations, stewardship turns out to be a rather enlightened anthropocentrism.[1] As

---

1. A considerable body of philosophical literature discusses whether the concept of obligations to future generations is ethically coherent. The following are representative (but by no means exhaustive) of this debate: Robin Attfield, "Beyond the Earth Charter: Taking Possible People Seriously," *Environmental Ethics* 29 (2007): 359–67; Brian Barry, "Sustainability and Intergenerational Justice," in *Environmental Ethics: An Anthology,* ed. Holmes Rolston III and Andrew Light (Oxford: Blackwell Publishing, 2003), 487–99; William J. FitzPatrick, "Climate Change and the Rights of Future Generations: Social Justice Beyond Mutual Advantage," *Environmental Ethics* 29 (2007): 369–88; Stephen M. Gardiner, "The Pure Intergenerational Problem," *The Monist* 86, no. 3 (2003): 481–500; Martin Golding, "Limited Obligations to Future Generations," *The Monist* 56 (1972): 85–99; Garrett Hardin, "Who Cares for Posterity?" in *The Limits of Altruism* (Indianapolis: Indiana University Press, 1977); Robert Heilbroner, "What Has Posterity Ever Done for Me?" *New York Times Magazine* (January 19, 1975); Derek Parfit, "Energy Policy and the Further Future: The Identity Problem," in *Climate Ethics: Essential Readings,* ed. Stephen M. Gardiner et al. (New York: Oxford University Press, 2010), 112–21.

the British ethicist Robin Attfield has noted, according to this model of stewardship each generation is responsible to the "transgenerational community" of humanity.

> It is inadequate to understand present agents as isolated individuals; without our ever having volunteered for membership, we seem to find ourselves involved as participants in a transgenerational community of moral agents, inheriting both benefits and burdens from our predecessors and passing them on to our successors. With regard to the environment, this suggests (if it is true) that we are entrusted by our forebears (whether or not they intend this) with the care of the planet and its systems, and that we perforce share this task with our successors, who will be among the beneficiaries if we play our part. In other words, we are trustees of the planet.[2]

Like Denethor, the present generation is the latest in a long line of stewards or trustees obligated to preserve and protect the natural world for present and future generations. However, unlike Tolkien's fictional scenario, no "ranger from the north" will one day return. This secular model of stewardship has no king. Each generation has an obligation to the transgenerational community of which it is a part to leave "as much and as good" as it inherited.[3] Notice that by framing stewardship exclusively in terms of obligations to present and future generations, this version of ecological stewardship essentially becomes a version of sustainability, which is often defined as meeting the needs of the present without compromising the ability of future generations to meet their needs.[4]

On the other hand, if one were to adopt a secular conception of ecological stewardship grounded in a biocentric or ecocentric conception of value, the scope of ecological stewardship is greatly

---

2. Robin Attfield, *The Ethics of the Global Environment* (West Lafayette, IN: Purdue University Press, 1999), 44–45.

3. This is the phrase used by John Locke in his *Second Treatise of Government*, ed. C. B. Macpherson (Indianapolis: Hackett, 1980).

4. I am grateful to my editor, Kathleen Walsh, for pointing this out. See chapter 4 for a more developed discussion of sustainability.

expanded. Indeed, a model of ecological stewardship that affirms the intrinsic value of all living organisms (biocentrism) and perhaps the systems of which they are a part (ecocentrism) recognizes that humans are answerable not merely to present and future humans, but to all the myriad forms of life that constitute the broader biotic community.

Religious Stewardship

Those who believe in a transcendent creator find it easier to address the notion of "answerability": as stewards of nature, humans answer to God. Again, like Denethor, the human community is the latest in a long line of stewards or trustees obligated to preserve and protect the natural world until the "return of the king," or God. As Attfield notes, according to the major monotheistic Abrahamic religious traditions of Judaism, Christianity, and Islam, "humanity is answerable to God, both for the use and for the care of nature, rather as the steward of an estate is answerable to its owner, or as trustees are answerable before the law for the goods which they hold on trust."[5] This view has a potentially dramatic effect on how one interprets the creation stories in general and the notion of dominion in particular, for in this view, Earth has not been given to humans to exploit for their own purposes; it has been entrusted to them to respect and protect.

The Christian Roots of the Ecological Crisis?

Despite their seeming compatibility with the stewardship model, some have argued that the Abrahamic religions cannot truly embrace this model because they define humanity's relationship to creation in terms of a divinely ordained despot.[6] Indeed, some have argued that Christianity in particular is inherently anthropocentric and that this anthropocentrism is the root cause of the current ecological crisis.

---

5. Attfield, *Ethics*, 45.

6. This section and the next are expanded versions of Brian G. Henning, "From Despot to Steward: The Greening of Catholic Social Teaching," in *The Heart of Catholic Social Teaching: Its Origins and Contemporary Significance*, ed. David Matzko McCarthy (Grand Rapids, MI: Brazos Press, 2009).

In a now-famous article titled "The Historical Roots of Our Ecologic Crisis," the historian Lynn White Jr. argues that Christianity deserves much of the blame for creating and perpetuating this destructive attitude toward nature. Though written decades ago, White's essay is still included in most environmental ethics texts today. To some ethicists it represents a compelling account of Christianity's role in creating the attitudes that made the ecological crisis possible.

White argues that how people interact with their environment is "deeply conditioned by beliefs about our nature and destiny—that is, by religion."[7] People's most basic beliefs inform their understanding of what they are allowed or not allowed to do to the natural environment. White notes that in antiquity, pagan animism held that "every tree, every spring, every stream, every hill had its own *genius loci*, its guardian spirit. . . . Before one cut a tree, mined a mountain, or dammed a brook, it was important to placate the spirit in charge of that particular situation, and to keep it placated."[8] Christianity, on the other hand, inherited from the Judaic tradition stories of creation in which God created humans, unique among creatures, in the divine image and gave them dominion over the created order (Gen 1:26–30).[9] When ancient paganism was supplanted, the idea of spirits in nature evaporated. The sacred grove becomes a mere stand of trees to use for fuel, and the holy mountain becomes a site for a new ski run. White argues, "Christianity, in absolute contrast

---

7. Lynn White Jr., "The Historical Roots of Our Ecologic Crisis," *Science* 155 (March 10, 1967): 1205. Many published works critique White's work. One of the first was written by Lewis W. Moncrief, "The Cultural Basis for Our Environmental Crisis: Judeo-Christian Tradition Is Only One of Many Cultural Factors Contributing to the Environmental Crisis," *Science* 170 (1970): 508–12. Moncrief writes, "The Judeo-Christian tradition has probably influenced the character of each of these forces. However, to isolate religious tradition as a cultural component and to contend that it is the 'historical root of our ecological crisis' is a bold affirmation for which there is little historical or scientific support" (51). One of the most thorough critiques is by Elspeth Whitney, "Lynn White, Ecotheology, and History," *Environmental Ethics* 15 (Summer 1993): 151–69. Despite these critiques, White's essay continues to be compelling to many ethicists.

8. White, "Historical Roots," 1205.

9. There are at least two different creation stories in Genesis. For a helpful discussion of the differences between the stories, see Mary Kate Birge, "Genesis," in *Genesis, Evolution, and the Search for a Reasoned Faith*, ed. Mary Kate Birge et al. (Winona, MN: Anselm Academic, 2011), 1–40.

to ancient paganism and Asia's religions, . . . not only established a dualism of man and nature but also insisted that it is God's will that man exploit nature for his proper ends."[10]

White acknowledges that Christianity is "a complex faith, and its consequences differ in differing contexts."[11] He notes, for instance, that the Eastern church has historically fostered a very different attitude toward nature. He also recognizes the alternative view of the relationship between humans and nature presented by Saint Francis, whom he calls "the greatest spiritual revolutionary in Western history . . . [because] he tried to substitute the idea of the equality of all creatures, including man, for the idea of man's limitless rule of creation."[12] The problem, White goes on to note, is that "he failed."[13] Thus White's basic claim is that the Western form of Christianity is the most anthropocentric religion the world has ever seen.[14] "God planned all of this explicitly for man's benefit and rule: no item in the physical creation had any purpose save to serve man's purposes. And, although man's body is made of clay, he is not simply part of nature: he is made in God's image."[15] Genesis 1 calls on humans to "subdue" Earth and to have "dominion" over every living creature (Gen 1:26–28). Christianity, according to White's interpretation, understood humans not as benevolent stewards but as divinely appointed despots over nature and thus created the underlying worldview that justifies the wasteful and indiscriminate destruction of the natural world. What should people today make of these claims that Christianity has created the attitudes that have led to the destruction of the environment? Is this a fair interpretation of Christianity and its sacred texts? It is important to distinguish White's *historical* claim regarding how the notion of dominion has been understood by Christians in the past from the *theological* claim regarding how best to interpret these passages in Genesis.

---

10. White, "Historical Roots," 1205.

11. Ibid., 1206.

12. Ibid., 1207.

13. Ibid.

14. Ibid., 1205.

15. Ibid., 1206.

Historically speaking, there does seem to be some merit in White's thesis.[16] As the ecotheologian James Nash puts it, "A satisfactory response to the ecological complaint against Christianity must begin with a forthright confession that at least much of the complaint is essentially true. Christianity does bear part of the burden of guilt for our ecological crisis. Ongoing repentance is warranted."[17] Historically speaking, Christians often embraced an arrogant anthropocentric view of nature that allowed the development of a destructive understanding of humanity's relationship to nature.[18] While there may be some support for White's *historical* argument, his claim that Christianity is *inherently* or *necessarily* anthropocentric is far less certain.[19]

As noted agrarian poet and author Wendell Berry acknowledges, "The conservationist indictment of Christianity [such as presented by White] is a problem . . . because, however just it may be, it does not come from an adequate understanding of the Bible and the cultural traditions that descend from the Bible."[20] Indeed, many contemporary theologians—not only Christian, but Jewish and Islamic as well—have begun to reexamine what it means to have "dominion" over creation.

---

16. White claims that it was the Western Christian views of nature that created the conditions for the possibility of the creation of technologies that reshaped the Earth in aggressive manners. Theologian Anne M. Clifford agrees with this historical claim to some degree, "A literal interpretation of Genesis 1 also had the potential of contributing to the exploitation of nonhuman nature. Directives to 'subdue' the earth and to have 'dominion' over every living creature (Gen 1:28) were applied uncritically to legitimate human domination of nonhuman nature, as if it were a right given to humans by God." "Foundations for a Catholic Ecological Theology of God," in *And God Saw that It Was Good: Catholic Theology and the Environment* (Washington, DC: United States Catholic Conference, 1996), 21.

17. James A. Nash, *Loving Nature: Ecological Integrity and Christian Responsibility* (Nashville, TN: Abingdon Press, 1991), 72.

18. Attfield argues that an explicit notion of stewardship first comes into Christianity in the work of John Calvin in the sixteenth century but that such stewardship did not apply to animals and the environment until the work of Hale in the seventeenth century. Attfield, *Ethics*, 50–51.

19. As indicated, White does not believe that Christianity is inherently anthropocentric or environmentally destructive. He lays the blame primarily on the Western form of Christianity.

20. Wendell Berry, "Christianity and the Survival of Creation," *Cross Currents* 43, no. 2 (Summer 1993), *www.crosscurrents.org/berry.htm*.

From Anthropocentrism to Theocentrism

Anne M. Clifford represents a growing number of Christian theologians placing a renewed emphasis on the proper understanding of the Genesis creation accounts. Clifford argues that understanding the true meaning of "dominion" requires considering it in the context of the story of the great flood.

> In chapter 6 [of Genesis], we find God deeply grieved about the extent of the wickedness of humans, precipitating an ecological disaster of worldwide proportions. . . . God's directive [to build an ark for all animals] makes the meaning of having dominion clear—it is to see the survival of the other living creatures. . . . The Noahic covenant is a symbol of the unbreakable bond between all creatures and their Creator.[21]

Understood within the context of the Noahic covenant, therefore, dominion does not give humans license to use nature with impunity. Rather, dominion carries the grave responsibility to care for and protect God's creation for present and future generations. The Bible does not justify exploitation of Earth and its many forms of plant and animal life. Indeed, such behavior breaks God's covenant with creation.

Similarly, rabbi Lawrence Troster recognizes that although the Torah states that humans are uniquely created in the image of God, this need not be at odds with modern environmentalism.[22] "Judaism always has valued the prohibition of the wanton destruction of nature. . . . Nonetheless, the 'image of God' concept does assert that human beings have a unique and dominant role in the world, even if it is as stewards and protectors of the earth."[23] Indeed, Troster goes on to note that within Judaism humans are seen as "partners" with God, finishing God's creation. "In this view, the

---

21. Clifford, "Foundations," 27.

22. Lawrence Troster, "Created in the Image of God: Humanity and Divinity in an Age of Environmentalism," in *Environmental Ethics: Divergence & Convergence*, 3rd ed., ed. Susan J. Armstrong and Richard G. Botzler (New York: McGrawHill, 2004), 225.

23. Ibid., 226.

world is unfinished, and human beings are empowered by God to complete God's work."[24] Given this view, Troster notes that within Judaism nature is *not* sacred; it is not intrinsically valuable. According to the Jewish tradition, "the world was created essentially for human benefit. Judaism does have an anthropocentric view of the world."[25] However, Troster explains, by being uniquely made in the image of the Creator, humans do have a special responsibility to care for the Earth, not for its own sake, but for the sake of its creator. A similar view can be found within Islam.

Mawil Y. Izzi Deen, a professor at King Abdul Aziz University in Saudi Arabia, argues that in the Qur'an "the conservation of the environment is based on the principle that all the individual components of the environment were created by God."[26] Thus Islam requires that Muslims' use of the environment avoids unnecessary destruction. Misuse of nature shows disrespect for its creator. Izzi Deen explains, "The environment is God's creation and to protect it is to preserve its values as a sign of the Creator."[27]

In each of these three religious interpretations of stewardship—Christian, Jewish, and Muslim—we find a common element: an immature, destructive anthropocentrism gives way before a more mature, nuanced **theocentrism** that recognizes that all meaning and value ultimately comes from the divine. Each item in creation only has meaning and value insofar as it relates to or comes from the divine being. In the context of Judaism, Christianity, and Islam, humans do not "own" Earth. A properly *theocentric* conception of dominion entails responsible ecological stewardship, not arrogant despotism.

Reconceiving Stewardship

Yet some environmental ethicists remain concerned that, as a moral framework, the stewardship model, in both its secular and religious forms, ultimately fails to shed fully its anthropocentrism because it

24. Ibid.

25. Ibid.

26. Mawil Y. Izzi Deen, "Islamic Environmental Ethics, Law, and Society," in *Environmental Ethics: Divergence & Convergence*, 3rd ed., ed. Susan J. Armstrong and Richard G. Botzler (New York: McGrawHill, 2004), 240.

27. Ibid.

still sets humans over nature as its caretakers or trustees.[28] The concern is that by retaining this kernel of anthropocentrism the stewardship model unintentionally feeds the narrative that humans are not only separate from nature, but set above and over a natural world that needs to be cared for and guarded. What some environmental ethicists question is whether this view of humans and their relationship to nature is scientifically warranted or ethically desirable.

It is not clear that the view of humans as benevolent caretakers of the planet (whether on behalf of an intergenerational community of humans, other living beings, or the divine) is supported by our current understanding of the cosmos and our place (and time) within it. Long ago Copernicus discovered that our little blue planet is not the center of the universe; it isn't even the center of our solar system. And Darwin revealed that humans are a part and product of a natural process that has created the many forms of life on Earth. Although many people intellectually recognize these truths, many of us don't emotionally accept them. As Lynn White puts it, "Despite Copernicus, all the cosmos rotates around our little globe. Despite Darwin, we are *not*, in our hearts, part of the natural process."[29] Fully coming to terms with the scientific meaning of contemporary cosmology and evolutionary biology requires that humans recognize that *no* version of anthropocentrism is justified. As White puts it, "We shall continue to have a worsening ecological crisis until we reject the Christian axiom that nature has no reason for existence save to serve man."[30] Humans are not an *exception to* the physical and biological forces that have shaped the natural world, but are rather an *exemplification of* these forces. Humans are a part of the natural world, not apart from it. Given this, it is not clear that it makes sense to claim that humans are responsible for, much less in charge of the planet.

Harvard University paleontologist Stephen Jay Gould (1941–2002) captured this point with characteristic flair:

> Such views, however well intentioned, are rooted in the old
> sin of pride and exaggerated self-importance. We are one

---

28. See, for instance, Clare Palmer, "Stewardship: A Case Study in Environmental Ethics," in *The Earth Beneath*, ed. J. Ball et al. (London: SPCK, 1992), 67–86.

29. White, "Historical Roots," 1206.

30. Ibid., 1207.

among millions of species, stewards of nothing. By what argument could we, arising just a geological microsecond ago, become responsible for the affairs of a world 4.5 billion years old, teeming with life that has been evolving and diversifying for at least three-quarters of that immense span? Nature does not exist for us, had no idea we were coming, and doesn't give a damn about us.[31]

Gould has an important, if somewhat exaggerated, point: by retaining an element of anthropocentrism, an invidious hubris has the potential to sneak into the hearts of even well-intentioned stewards. *Homo sapiens* are a truly impressive species, but humans are also a very young species, having only arrived on the evolutionary scene a few hundred thousand years ago, a "geological microsecond" in the 4.5-billion-year history of the planet. According to this view, the idea that nature or the planet needs to be taken care of is, however well intentioned, rooted "in the old sin of pride and exaggerated self-importance."[32]

Perhaps in this ecological context the idea of stewardship needs to be reconceived. If humans *are* stewards, perhaps it is *not* in the way that a gardener maintains a Victorian rose garden.[33] For Earth does not exist solely for the benefit of humans. Further, perhaps humans aren't benevolent leaders of nature. For whereas the people of Gondor needed someone to protect and to lead them, this does not seem to be the case with the natural world, which often flourishes more when humans simply get out of the way. But does recognition of these points mean that the concept of ecological stewardship is so flawed that it should be abandoned entirely? Perhaps not. Perhaps the concept can be applied not to nature, but to the human community itself. That is, perhaps what is needed to respond to the growing reality of global climate disruption is not for humans to become gardening stewards cultivating nature. Perhaps what is needed is a form of *self-stewardship* that makes it possible for humans to become responsible *citizens* of the wider biotic community.

---

31. Stephen Jay Gould, "The Golden Rule—A Proper Scale for Our Environmental Crisis," *Natural History* 99, no. 9 (September 1990): 24.

32. Ibid.

33. The metaphor of stewardship as "gardeners" is defended by John Houghton, *Global Warming: The Complete Briefing*, 4th ed. (Cambridge: Cambridge University Press, 2009), 250–51.

As the iconoclastic scientist James Lovelock notes,

> We are creatures of Darwinian evolution, a transient species with a limited lifespan, as were all our numerous distant ancestors. But, unlike almost everything before we emerged on the planet, we are also intelligent, social animals with the possibility of evolving to become a wiser and more intelligent animal, one that might have a greater potential as a partner for the rest of life on Earth.[34]

The idea of partnership is central to this more humble notion of self-stewardship. But this is not a partnership in which humans finish creation, as Troster described. Rather, what is implied is an ecological partnership. A chastened notion of human self-stewardship would recognize that humans are but one among millions of beautiful forms of life in a universe some 13.75 billion years old. Accordingly, humanity's task is *not* to become managers of the planet, but to become responsible stewards of itself, to pursue ways of living that make it possible for humans to find a harmonious place within the biotic community. As the eminent cultural historian Thomas Berry (1914–2009) has argued, this reconceiving of what it is to be human is the "Great Work" of our historical age.[35]

The Great Work and the Ecozoic Era

Berry contends that each historical age is defined by the challenges with which its time and place confront it. The success or failure of each age hinges on whether that generation takes up the "Great Work" demanded of those challenges. Berry believes that today humanity is at a particularly significant point in history. Anthropogenic global climate change and the prospect of a sixth mass extinction are greater challenges than anything our species has faced before. Confronting these challenges is the great work of this historical age. Those of us born at this moment in time did not chose this work, but it is ours nonetheless.

---

34. James Lovelock, *The Vanishing Face of Gaia: A Final Warning* (New York: Basic Books, 2009), 9.

35. Thomas Berry, *The Great Work: Our Way into the Future* (New York: Three Rivers Press, 1999).

It is easy to lose sight of the magnitude of what Berry is suggesting. It is not enough to tinker around the edges, putting up solar panels here and wind mills there, though these actions are needed. For Berry, to successfully take up the great work before us requires nothing short of a reconsideration of what it is to be human. "The historical mission of our times is to reinvent the human—at the species level, with critical reflection, within the community of life-systems, in a time-developmental context, by means of story and shared dream experience."[36] *This* is the great work for people today: *to figure out how to conceive of humanity as an integral part of the natural world.* In a sense, the task of our historical age is to give up the pretense of anthropocentrism and meaningfully join the Earth community.

Thomas Berry's great work and the "land ethic" of the renowned naturalist Aldo Leopold (1887–1948), who wrote a half-century earlier, are similar in striking ways.[37] Leopold argues that in the course of human history the boundaries of the moral community have gradually expanded beyond the narrow boundaries of one's family, tribe, city, and nation, and, more recently, beyond one's gender and race. He sees this expansion of the moral community as a movement of ethical evolution.[38] The problem, he notes, is that ethics still excludes the natural world from the moral community. Thus the next stage of ethical evolution of humanity, Leopold contends, is the development of a "land ethic" that "enlarges the boundaries of the community to include soils, waters, planets, and animals, or collectively: the land."[39]

---

36. Ibid., 159.

37. There is insufficient space here to develop this claim further. It is important to note that scholars such as J. Baird Callicott, perhaps the most respected commentator on Leopold's work, would not necessarily agree with the interpretation given here. For a representation of Callicott's view of Leopold, see J. Baird Callicott, *In Defense of the Land Ethic: Essays in Environmental Philosophy* (Albany: State University of New York Press, 1989). For an alternative environmental ethic inspired by Leopold, see Holmes Rolston III, *Environmental Ethics: Duties to and Values in the Natural World* (Philadelphia: Temple University Press, 1988). Finally, for my own defense of an ethic broadly inspired by Leopold that takes the third of the triad—integrity, stability, beauty—as the central moral category, see Henning, *The Ethics of Creativity: Beauty, Morality, and Nature in a Processive Cosmos* (Pittsburgh, PA: University of Pittsburgh Press, 2005); and Brian G. Henning, "Trusting in the 'Efficacy of Beauty': A Kalocentric Approach to Moral Philosophy," *Ethics & the Environment* 14, no .1 (2009): 101–28.

38. Aldo Leopold, "The Land Ethic," in *A Sand County Almanac and Sketches Here and There* (New York: Oxford University Press, [1949] 1987), 202–3.

39. Ibid., 204.

However, there is at present a logjam in the ethical evolutionary stream that is impeding this development. The "key-log,"[40] Leopold writes, that must be removed to "release the evolutionary process" is simply this: "quit thinking about decent land use as solely an economic problem."[41] Leopold is *not* suggesting that this ethic would require that humans never make use of nature.[42] On the contrary, he is merely saying that humanity must not see its relationship to the wider biotic community *merely* in terms of what is economically expedient. All living beings modify their environment as they pursue their ends. But as a member of a wide "biotic community" that includes the air, the soil, waters, animals, plants, and humans, we should examine each situation not only relative to what is "economically expedient" but *also* "in terms of what is ethically and esthetically right."[43] In this way, Leopold arrives at his fundamental moral principle: "A thing is right when it tends to preserve the integrity, stability, and beauty of the biotic community. It is wrong when it tends otherwise."[44] Though consistent with the concepts of sustainability and stewardship, Leopold's principle is arguably more capacious, in that moral action should aim not only to maintain the integrity and stability of nature but also respect its beauty. The development of this land ethic, which recognizes the value of every member of the biotic community, is, Leopold believes, "an evolutionary possibility and an ecological necessity."[45] That is, it is *possible* for humanity to grow out of its childish anthropocentrism and develop a wider land ethic and, given the dire state of the biotic community, it is ecologically *necessary* it do so.

Thus both Berry and Leopold contend that a primary goal of ethics should be to foster an intense consciousness of this interdependence, to extend humanity's concept of community to recognize that

---

40. Prior to the development of other means, loggers floated cut trees on rivers to lumber mills downstream. At times, this would create a "logjam." The "key-log" is that log which, if removed, would relieve the logjam, allowing the flow to proceed. Leopold is using the idea of the logjam and the key-log as a metaphor for ethical evolution.

41. Leopold, "Land Ethic," 224.

42. Leopold writes, "A land ethic of course cannot prevent the alteration, management, and use of these 'resources,' but it does affirm their right to continued existence, and, at least in spots, their continued existence in a natural state." Ibid., 204.

43. Ibid., 224.

44. Ibid.

45. Ibid., 203.

we are already a part of the wider natural world. Clearly, according to this, view humans stop seeing themselves as conquerors of the land, but perhaps it also requires that they stop seeing themselves as stewards who are in charge of nature. Berry contends, "We misconceive our role if we consider that our historical mission is to 'civilize' or to 'domesticate' the planet, as though wildness is something destructive rather than the ultimate creative modality of any form of earthly being. We are not here to control. We are here to become integral with the larger Earth community."[46] For both Leopold and Berry, the great work demanded of the present generation is to but become an integral and benign member of the biotic community. This cannot be achieved merely by modifying "some specific aspect of our ethical conduct" or even a wholesale "modification of our existing cultural context." The needed change goes far beyond this. "What is demanded of us now is to change attitudes that are so deeply bound into our basic cultural patterns that they seem to us as imperative of the very nature of our being, a dictate of our genetic coding as a species."[47]

To illustrate the magnitude of the changes needed, Berry argues that we find ourselves not merely at the end a geological epoch (the Holocene)[48] but the end of a geological era (the Cenozoic Era).[49] The great work before humanity is not merely to mitigate the damage done by the Anthropocene but to usher in what Berry calls the "Ecozoic Era."

> Our own special role, which we will hand on to our children, is that of managing the arduous transition from the terminal Cenozoic to the emerging Ecozoic Era, the period when humans will be present to the planet as participating members of the comprehensive Earth community. This is our Great Work and the work of our children.[50]

---

46. Berry, *The Great Work*, 48.

47. Ibid., 105.

48. See also chapter 1 for a discussion of the Holocene and the Anthropocene.

49. Earth scientists divide geological history into various units, each of which is further subdivided. One of the bigger units is eon, which can cover hundreds of millions of years. The current eon is the Phanerozoic Eon, which began approximately 541 million years ago. Eons are divided into eras. The current era, known as the Cenozoic, began some 66 million years ago. Each era is subdivided into periods and epochs. So, we are currently in the Holocene Epoch of the Quaternary Period of the Cenozoic Era.

50. Berry, *The Great Work*, 7–8.

It is in this context of the great work and the emergence of a land ethic that one could conceive of a robust form of self-stewardship. According to such a view, the task before this generation is for humans to reconceive of themselves and their place within the biotic community—not as leaders of nature, but as self-stewards who seek humbly and fallibly to take a benign place within it.

Berry and Leopold forecast a worsening ecological crisis until such time as humans see their relationship to the land not only in economic terms but also and fundamentally as an ethical relationship. Humanity must learn to live in harmony and balance with the natural world, rather than dominate and exploit it: "In short, a land ethic changes the role of *Homo sapiens* from conqueror of the land-community to plain member and citizen of it. It implies respect for his fellow members, and also respect of the community as such."[51]

Becoming good stewards of humanity's impact on nature and finding a harmonious relationship with the biotic community will require that humanity fundamentally change how it conceives of a flourishing life, of the "good life." Self-stewardship encourages the development of an ethic that shifts the emphasis from "managing nature" for human use and stresses changing one's lifestyles to foster a flourishing human life *and* a vital natural world. As Pope John Paul II noted in 1990, "Modern society will find no solution to the ecological problem unless it *takes a serious look at its life style*."[52] This entails new ways of thinking and acting grounded in a re-envisioned relationship between humanity and the world—a fundamental shift in humanity's understanding of the life well lived. This demands more than merely internalizing environmental externalities and deploying more green technology. It raises questions about the consumer culture and its often-facile notions of success, beauty, and the good life.

Voluntary Simplicity

In their provocative essay "The Death of Environmentalism," Michael Shellenberger and Ted Nordhaus contend that the modern environmental movement has failed because it has focused on narrow

51. Leopold, "Land Ethic," 240.

52. Pope John Paul II, "Peace with God the Creator, Peace with All of Creation," January 1, 1990, *http://bit.ly/1nsMbbQ*, emphasis in original.

policy prescriptions grounded in economic models that define the good in terms of rational self-interest. Sullenberger and Nordhaus argue that this approach has focused too much attention on what environmentalism is *against* and not enough on what it is *for*.[53] Environmentalism is against fossil-fuels-based transportation and energy, against polluting water ways, against species extinction, against the oil pipeline. But, they argue, environmentalists don't spend enough time discussing what it is that they are for.

In discussions of the environment generally and climate change in particular, one often gets the impression that the best that can be done is merely to cause less harm, be less bad (e.g., by reducing one's carbon footprint). In framing itself in this negative way, environmentalism has failed to create a robust, *positive* vision that might inspire a transformation of society toward more meaningful ways of living. The environmental movement has, over the last forty years, focused more on educating people about the devastating effects of human pollution than sketching an alternative vision of how to live. Pictures of inundated coastlines and stories of devastating storms can be effective in getting people's attention. However, as important as awareness building and environmental education are, they do not offer a sufficient foundation for the long-term, intergenerational changes needed to restore balance to the climate or an adequate ethic for guidance on how to live in harmony with nature. Fear of environmental devastation—bigger storms, rising seas, mass extinctions, frequent drought, environmental refugees—though perhaps justified, does not provide a sufficient basis for the great work before us.

Fear is a useful evolutionary development for addressing immediate problems. Fear saved human ancestors from being eaten by bigger and faster animals and has been successfully used to marshal countries to respond to an imminent military threat. Though the likely impact of climate change will ultimately be more significant than that of a war, the changes it brings will extend over decades and centuries. People simply cannot remain

---

53. Michael Shellenberger and Ted Nordhaus, "The Death of Environmentalism: Global Warming Politics in a Post-Environmental World," The Breakthrough Institute, June 16, 2010, *http://bit.ly/ScPdTf*. Shellenberger and Nordhaus argue that "the environmental movement's failure to craft inspiring and powerful proposals to deal with global warming is directly related to the movement's reductive logic about the supposedly root causes (e.g., 'too much carbon in the atmosphere') of any given environmental problem" (14–15).

afraid for years. Like those who live in war-torn countries, after the initial shock has subsided, most people largely revert back to their ordinary habits.

Similarly (though perhaps a welcome development), the sustainability paradigm advocated by many within the environmental movement shows moral neutrality; it presupposes an understanding of the good life, rather than providing one.[54] That is, it presupposes that the good life is sufficiently defined by economic success and material acquisition. The environmental movement has done little to craft a compelling account of what a deeply sustainable life would look like; beyond the employment of new forms of green energy, the good life is assumed to be much the same as it is today. Some businesses have exploited the vacuum created by the failure to provide an alternative vision for the good life. Many even imply that humans need not change their lifestyles at all but can keep on as before, provided they change some light bulbs and buy a hybrid car. Those who do advocate living more lightly on the land are often ridiculed as anti-technology. Marketers suggest that *either* one can choose to live within modern society and pursue the materialistic notions of success that it embodies *or* one can reject modern society completely. This is likely a **false dilemma**.

To live in harmony with the larger biotic community, it is likely that humans will need to pursue an alternative vision of human flourishing based on something more than fear of future harm and the perpetual pursuit of economic wealth.[55] However, mixed reactions greet the suggestion that a shift in lifestyle is needed to successfully respond to the threats posed by global climate change. On the one hand, those in developed nations often live a fairly comfortable life, and giving up these luxuries sounds neither easy nor appealing. On the other hand, many of these same people also recognize that a life dedicated to the pursuit of wealth, prestige, and physical beauty is

---

54. See chapter 4's discussion of sustainability.

55. Philip Cafaro is a notable exception to the trend of suggesting a false dichotomy. Cafaro argues that "the push toward economic and ecological good sense" should include "specifying alternative visions of flourishing human lives and societies based on the full development of our human capabilities, rather than on ever-increasing wealth. . . . Here philosophers can link up with some very interesting work being done by positive psychologists like Time Kasser (2003), Richard Layard (2005) and Ed Diener (Diener and Biswas-Diener 2008)." Philip Cafaro, "Taming Growth and Articulating a Sustainable Future: The Way Forward for Environmental Ethics," *Ethics & the Environment* 16, no. 1 (Spring 2011): 14.

ultimately unfulfilling. Those who take social and environmental challenges seriously recognize the need for a change of lifestyle but often do not have a clear sense of how to accomplish it. They realize that purchasing Energy Star appliances, recycling, changing to LED light fixtures, eating less meat, and buying an electric or hybrid vehicle are not nearly enough to keep the planet below 2°C (3.6°F) warming this century. Stabilizing the climate and avoiding the most devastating results of global warming requires more significant change. Those in the developed nations ought to change their lifestyle in order to reduce greenhouse gas emissions, but what exactly would this new lifestyle look like?

Since the late 1970s, the social scientist and author Duane Elgin has conducted social scientific research on different models of human living. He has concluded that living a life of "voluntary simplicity" is not only necessary for avoiding catastrophic climate change but also can be much "richer," if one is willing to expand the conception of riches beyond the pursuit of material wealth. Elgin first started his research while working on his father's farm in Idaho with people who "lived on the edge of subsistence."[56] He realized that a life of voluntary simplicity differs greatly from a life of poverty.

> As I worked side by side with these fine people, I saw that poverty has a very human face—one that is very different from "simplicity." Poverty is involuntary and debilitating, whereas simplicity is voluntary and enabling. Poverty is mean and degrading to the human spirit, whereas a life of conscious simplicity can have both a beauty and a functional integrity that elevates the human spirit. Involuntary poverty generates a sense of helplessness, passivity, and despair, whereas purposeful simplicity fosters a sense of personal empowerment, creative engagement, and opportunity. Historically those choosing a simpler life have sought the golden mean—a creative and aesthetic balance between poverty and excess.[57]

Leading a life of voluntary simplicity means focusing on what will bring genuine and more-enduring forms of happiness and success:

---

56. Duane Elgin, *Voluntary Simplicity: Toward a Way of Life that Is Outwardly Simple, Inwardly Rich*, 2nd ed. (New York: Harper, 2010), 18.

57. Ibid., 19.

meaningful work that is worth doing, time with family and friends, and time in nature. In a sense, Elgin urges a balance similar to that which Aristotle advocated.[58] The ancient Greek philosopher argued that to achieve true happiness (what he called *eudaimonia*), one must seek ways of fulfilling every aspect of human potential. Pleasure, wealth, beauty, and power, though useful, do not bring authentic happiness. Genuine, enduring human flourishing requires the fulfillment of not only one's physical nature but also the mental, emotional, and social natures.

Elgin rightly notes that mainstream media, particularly advertisers, often misrepresent a life of voluntary simplicity as a regression:

> Simplicity is frequently presented as antitechnology and anti-innovation, a backward way of life that seeks a romantic return to a bygone era. . . . Seen in this way, simplicity is a cartoon lifestyle that seems naive, disconnected, and irrelevant—an approach to living that can be easily dismissed as impractical and unworkable.[59]

The misrepresentation makes it easier to maintain the status quo.[60] Although contrary to the current of consumer societies, choosing a balanced life of simplicity is not an anti-technology, "back to the land" movement but the conscious decision to seek happiness in friends, family, meaningful work, and time in nature.[61]

---

58. See Aristotle's *Nicomachean Ethics*, http://classics.mit.edu/Aristotle/nicomachaen.html.

59. Elgin, *Voluntary Simplicity*, 7.

60. Ibid., 8.

61. Elgin writes, "The romanticized image of rural living does not fit the modern reality, as a majority of persons choosing a life of conscious simplicity do not live in the backwoods or rural settings; they live in cities and suburbs. While green living brings with it a reverence for nature, that does not require moving to a rural setting. Instead of a "back to the land" movement, it is much more accurate to describe this as a "make the most of wherever you are" movement—and increasingly that means adapting ourselves creatively to a rapidly changing world in the context of big cities and suburbs" (ibid., 20). Philosopher Lester Milbrath says, "Simplicity is not turning away from progress; it is crucial to progress. It should not be equated with isolation and withdrawal from the world; most who choose this way of life build a personal network of people who share a similar intention. It also should not be equated with living in a rural setting; it is a 'make the most of wherever we are' movement. Voluntary simplicity would evolve both the material and conscious aspects of life in balance with each other—allowing each aspect to infuse and inform the other." "Redefining the Good Life in a Sustainable Society," *Environmental Values* 2, no. 3 (August 1993): 269.

There is, in Elgin's view, "no fixed or predetermined way to live simply; Earth-friendly living is something we are each challenged to invent in the unique circumstances of our individual lives."[62] Each person must find the appropriate balance. Thus although voluntary simplicity will involve fundamental changes to one's life and how one defines a life well lived, seeking such a life does not equate to a life of sacrifice and self-denial.

TABLE 5.1

Sacrifice[63]	Simplicity
• is a consumer lifestyle that is overstressed, overbusy, and overworked • is investing long hours doing work that is neither meaningful nor satisfying • is being apart from family and community to earn a living • is being cut off from nature's beauty • is the lack of opportunity for soulful encounters with others • is a hard, ascetic life	• cuts through needless busyness, clutter, and complications • is doing well, work that is well worth doing • keeps our eyes on what matters most—family, friends, community, nature, and the cosmos • fosters harmonious relationships with the biotic community • yields more lasting satisfaction, instead of often fleeting pleasures of consumerism • is a rich, aesthetic life

A lifestyle change toward voluntary simplicity entails a rejection of the economic logic that suggests that **standard of living**, defined in terms of wealth, comfort, and material goods, accurately measures quality of life. Material wealth and success are essential for providing the food, shelter, and medical treatment needed to live, but does additional wealth lead to a corresponding increase in happiness? The ethicist Philip Cafaro questions this assumption:

Studies have repeatedly shown that while increasing wealth in poor countries does augment happiness, once a society

62. Elgin, *Voluntary Simplicity*, 71.

63. Ibid., 4–6.

becomes sufficiently prosperous, further increases in wealth no longer boost subjective well-being. . . . Throughout the world, the cutoff line seems to be around $10,000, far below the average American income. Meanwhile, psychological studies show that a materialistic *outlook* is actually an impediment to individuals achieving happiness. . . . This is partly because such an outlook interferes with highly valuing people, and good relationships with spouses, friends, and co-workers turn out to be very important in securing happiness. All in all, there is little evidence that doubling our wealth will increase Americans' happiness or flourishing.[64]

My own experience bears this out. For years my spouse had been working full time at a neighboring university while also working on her dissertation. Between the demands of children, jobs, and schoolwork, we scarcely saw each other before collapsing into bed each night, exhausted. After much deliberation and some careful planning, we decided to have her quit her job to be a full-time mother and graduate student. This decision meant losing nearly 50% of our income. Thus economically, our standard of living fell by about half, which some might argue would lead to a corresponding drop in our quality of life. However, we did not find this to be the case.

Although we went without expensive vacations and eating out regularly, in nearly every other way the *quality* of our lives has dramatically improved. My spouse has time to volunteer at our daughters' schools; she has at long last finished her doctoral dissertation; and we spend considerably more time together. In short, our lives are less complicated and more meaningful. We are, quite simply, happier. But how is this possible if our "standard of living" has dropped by nearly 50%? I have found firsthand that a life simple in means can be very rich in ends. Such a life is not a hard, austere, ascetic life of self-denial. The philosopher Lester Milbrath puts this point well:

> To live with *simplicity* is not an ascetic but rather an aesthetic simplicity because it is consciously chosen; in doing so we unburden our lives to live more lightly, cleanly, and

---

64. Philip Cafaro, "Economic Growth or the Flourishing Life: The Ethical Choice Climate Change Puts to Humanity," *Essays in Philosophy* 11, no. 1 (2010): 15.

aerodynamically. Each person chooses a pattern or level of consumption to fit with grace and integrity into the practical art of daily living on this planet. We must learn the difference between those material circumstances that support our lives and those that constrict our lives.[65]

Discovering an elegant life of voluntary simplicity may be a critical element of successfully taking up the great work confronting humanity. If such a shift in attitudes and practices were to become prevalent, it might not only mitigate some of the worst consequences of global climate change but also lead to richer, more meaningful lives. In this way, voluntary simplicity is one among many ways that environmentalists might begin to move beyond the negative framing of our ecological challenges and frame positive visions of a better future. Being *for* a rich and meaningful life of voluntary simplicity goes far beyond just being *against* carbon pollution.

In sum, the concepts of deep sustainability and self-stewardship can be useful if they help push beyond a tacit anthropocentrism. The world does not exist solely for the sake of humans, and it does not need human caretakers to flourish. Given the scale of human impacts, humans must humbly become good stewards of *themselves* and seek forms of living compatible with a thriving natural world. We are at a pivotal point in the history of our species. The ecological crisis may create the needed catalyst for humans to begin to see themselves as a part of the wider Earth community.

As chapter 6 discusses, the notions of great work, deep sustainability, voluntary simplicity, and self-stewardship do not set out a particular moral code or set of moral laws but offer moral ideals to pursue. The moral life entails constructing forms of living that will make it possible for humans to take their place within—not above or over—the biotic community. Creating this new moral awareness is critical if humanity is not to merely survive but thrive in the changing climate that it has created.

---

65. Milbrath, "Redefining the Good Life," 268–69. Elgin says, "Rather than involving a denial of beauty, simplicity liberates the *aesthetic* sense by freeing things from artificial encumbrances. From a spiritual perspective, simplicity removes the obscuring clutter and discloses the spirit that infuses all things." *Voluntary Simplicity*, 20.

For Further Exploration

1. In the final analysis, do you find that the concept of ecological stewardship retains an element of anthropocentrism? Why or why not? Do you find this to be a strength or weakness of the position? Explain.

2. Identify times when you have been happiest. Beyond a certain level, can the pursuit of material wealth and possessions constitute full happiness? If you were to define it for yourself and chose to pursue it, what would a life simple in means and rich in ends look like?

3. After watching the video *The Story of Stuff* (*http://storyofstuff .org/*) and the PBS video *Affluenza* (*www.pbs.org/kcts/affluenza /home.html*; a clip of the one-hour video is at *www.youtube.com /watch?v=xlNAJm4FTVY*), consider whether or to what degree consumption makes human beings meaningfully happy.

4. Define for yourself the notion of "success." Now, explore how society or popular culture defines success. Do the two accounts coincide? Why or why not?

Additional Resources

OBLIGATIONS TO FUTURE GENERATIONS

Attfield, Robin. "Beyond the Earth Charter: Taking Possible People Seriously." *Environmental Ethics* 29 (2007): 359–67.

Barry, Brian. "Sustainability and Intergenerational Justice." In *Environmental Ethics: An Anthology*, edited by Holmes Rolston III and Andrew Light, 487–99. Oxford: Blackwell Publishing, 2003.

FitzPatrick, William J. "Climate Change and the Rights of Future Generations: Social Justice Beyond Mutual Advantage." *Environmental Ethics* 29 (2007): 369–88.

Gardiner, Stephen M. "The Pure Intergenerational Problem." *The Monist* 86, no. 3 (2003): 481–500.

Golding, Martin. "Limited Obligations to Future Generations." *The Monist* 56 (1972): 85–99.

Hardin, Garrett. "Who Cares for Posterity?" In *The Limits of Altruism*. Indianapolis: Indiana University Press, 1977.

Heilbroner, Robert. "What Has Posterity Ever Done for Me?" *New York Times Magazine*, January 19, 1975.

Parfit, Derek. "Energy Policy and the Further Future: The Identity Problem." In *Climate Ethics: Essential Readings*, edited by Stephen M. Gardiner, Simon Caney, Dale Jamieson, and Henry Shue, 112–21. New York: Oxford University Press, 2010.

STEWARDSHIP AND ECOLOGICAL ETHICS

Attfield, Robin. *The Ethics of the Global Environment*. West Lafayette, IN: Purdue University Press, 1999.

Berry, Thomas. *The Great Work: Our Way into the Future*. New York: Three Rivers Press, 1999.

Christiansen, Drew, and Walter Grazer, eds. *"And God Saw that It Was Good": Catholic Theology and the Environment*. Washington, DC: United States Conference of Catholic Bishops, 1996.

Gould, Stephen Jay. "The Golden Rule—A Proper Scale for Our Environmental Crisis." *Natural History* 99, no. 9 (September 1990).

Henning, Brian G. "From Despot to Steward: The Greening of Catholic Social Teaching." In *The Heart of Catholic Social Teaching: Its Origins and Contemporary Significance*, edited by David Matzko McCarthy. Grand Rapids, MI: Brazos Press, 2009.

Nash, James A. *Loving Nature: Ecological Integrity and Christian Responsibility*. Nashville, TN: Abingdon Press, 1991.

Palmer, Clare. "Stewardship: A Case Study in Environmental Ethics." In *The Earth Beneath*, edited by Ian Ball, Margaret Goodall, Clare Palmer, and John Reader, 67–86. London: SPCK, 1992.

ALDO LEOPOLD'S "THE LAND ETHIC"

Callicott, J. Baird. *In Defense of the Land Ethic: Essays in Environmental Philosophy*. Albany: State University of New York Press, 1989.
Callicot is one of the leading experts on Leopold.

———. *Thinking Like a Planet: The Land Ethic and the Earth Ethic*. New York: Oxford University Press, 2014.

Henning, Brian G. *The Ethics of Creativity: Beauty, Morality, and Nature in a Processive Cosmos.* Pittsburgh: University of Pittsburgh Press, 2005.
My own defense of an ethic broadly inspired by Leopold.

———. "Trusting in the 'Efficacy of Beauty': A Kalocentric Approach to Moral Philosophy." *Ethics & the Environment* 14, no. 1 (2009): 101–28.

Leopold, Aldo. *A Sand County Almanac and Sketches Here and There.* New York: Oxford University Press, [1949] 1987.

Rolston, Holmes, III. *Environmental Ethics: Duties to and Values in the Natural World.* Philadelphia: Temple University Press, 1988.
A classic work by one of the founders of modern environmental ethics.

WESTERN CHRISTIANITY'S PART IN THE ECOLOGICAL CRISIS

Moncrief, Lewis W. "The Cultural Basis for Our Environmental Crisis: Judeo-Christian Tradition Is Only One of Many Cultural Factors Contributing to the Environmental Crisis." *Science* 170 (1970): 508–12.

White, Lynn, Jr. "The Historical Roots of Our Ecologic Crisis." *Science* 155 (March 10, 1967).

Whitney, Elspeth. "Lynn White, Ecotheology, and History." *Environmental Ethics* 15 (Summer 1993): 151–69.

SIMPLICITY MOVEMENT

Alexander, Samuel, et al. *Voluntary Simplicity: The Poetic Alternative to Consumer Culture.* New Zealand: Stead & Daughters, 2009.

de Graaf, John, et al. *Affluenza: The All-Consuming Epidemic.* 2nd ed. San Francisco: Berrett-Koehler Publishers, 2005.

Elgin, Duane. *Voluntary Simplicity: Toward a Way of Life that Is Outwardly Simple, Inwardly Rich.* 2nd ed. New York: Harper, 2010.

Milbrath, Lester. "Redefining the Good Life in a Sustainable Society." *Environmental Values* 2, no. 3 (August 1993): 261–69.

Simple Living Institute, *www.simplelivinginstitute.org/.*
Helpful tips and resources.

Simplicity Institute, *http://simplicityinstitute.org/.*
A non-profit education and research center founded by Samuel Alexander and Simon Ussher dedicated to advancing the Simplicity Movement.

Moral Idealism, Hypocrisy, and Pursuit of the Great Work

Previous chapters argued that successfully addressing the many challenges created by a changing climate requires a deeper conception of sustainability and a humbler notion of stewardship that together re-envision how humans see themselves and their relationship to the natural environment. This vision shifts the moral ideal from reducing the impact of a late-stage consumer society (shallow sustainability) to the transformation of humans into responsible citizens of the global biotic community (self-stewardship) who seek happiness in a life of voluntary simplicity (deep sustainability). Bringing about this transformation of humanity and its relationship to nature is the great work of this historical age.

Some might object that it is difficult to see how to move from an anthropocentric society built on consumption and perpetual growth to a human community respecting the value of all life-forms and defining success in qualitative terms of happiness rather than quantitative measures of wealth and consumption. Exactly how this transition will take place and whether it can be implemented quickly enough to avoid catastrophic climate change is not at all clear. This chapter will consider two common objections often leveled against those who might attempt to take up this great work: (1) such approaches are hopelessly idealistic, and (2) those who pursue these lofty ideals hypocritically betray their beliefs through their actions.

Be Realistic

Many people realize that the threat of global climate change is real and growing.[1] They also see that a fundamental shift toward living more simply and in harmony with nature might not only begin to address this threat but also lead to more humane and fulfilling lives. But as desirable as these things are, aren't they just too idealistic? We have serious challenges to face. We must be realistic. The students in my classes often present this sort of view—and for good reason. The generations before them have left quite a mess, and addressing the situation seems overwhelming and nearly impossible.

In his essay "Good Enough," the respected philosopher John Lachs argues that grounding moral frameworks in unachievable moral ideals is not only philosophically misguided but also psychologically damaging.

> The perverse desire to heap infinite obligations on finite individuals guarantees moral failure. Similarly, demanding perfection of our experiences and relationships is a certain way of making life miserable. We do much better if we heed the counsels of finitude and refuse to seek what cannot be obtained. This involves both judgment and resolve: we must be able to decide what is good enough and willing to embrace it as sufficient for our purposes; that is, adequate to satisfy our desires. The romantic quest for the perfect destroys human relationships and converts what could be happy lives into the misery of endless seeking and striving.[2]

Instead of pursuing an unachievable ideal, Lachs argues for the principle of "good enough." In many ways, Lachs's concept of "good enough" is quite similar to the notion of "voluntary simplicity" discussed in chapter 5. It is vital that people develop the ability to be satisfied by what is good enough instead of always aspiring for ever more. However, note that Lachs's argument goes further, suggesting

---

1. This section on ideals is adapted from Brian G. Henning, "Sustainability and Other Ecological Mistakes," in *Beyond Superlatives*, ed. Roland Faber, J. R. Hustwit, and Hollis Phelps (Newcastle upon Tyne: Cambridge Scholars Press, 2014): 76–89.

2. John Lachs, "Good Enough," *Journal of Speculative Philosophy* 23, no. 1 (2009): 1.

that if one is to be satisfied by what is good enough, one must reject the pursuit of unachievable moral ideals.

> As affirmation of our finitude, it [what is good enough] negates our Faustian tendency to want to have and do everything. It rejects the relevance of the ideal of perfection and strikes at the root of our compulsion to pursue unreachable ideals. It liberates us to the enjoyment of the possible without eliminating standards or moral effort. It enables us to still our will by achieving what we can and celebrating what we do.[3]

Lachs notes that his position does not require one to settle "for the dregs or live a compromise accepting shoddy goods."[4] Rather, he argues, those satisfied by what is "good enough" can then "enjoy what is fine and permit themselves to feel fulfilled, refusing to search for some elusive ideal."[5]

Given Lachs's argument as context, how might one respond to those who counsel realism despite generally agreeing with the desirability of moral frameworks such as deep sustainability and self-stewardship? The implicit premises behind this sort of argument might look something like the following:

1. Moral framework P is either realistic or idealistic but never both.
2. P is realistic if its ends are achievable.
3. P is idealistic if its ends cannot be fully achieved.
4. Only moral frameworks with achievable ends ought to be pursued.
5. Therefore, one ought not to adopt P if it is idealistic.[6]

In other words, the argument claims that because only moral frameworks with achievable ends should be pursued (premise 4), and the ends of idealistic moral frameworks are, by definition, not

---

3. Ibid., 7.

4. Ibid., 2.

5. Ibid.

6. My thanks to David Kovacs for his help with this argument reconstruction.

achievable (premise 3); people should not adopt idealistic moral frameworks. Instead, they should be realistic by pursuing moral frameworks with achievable ends (premise 2).

Contrary to what one might expect, the problem with this argument is not with the third premise. By definition, true moral ideals are *not* fully achievable. Rather, the problem lies with the fourth premise—the claim that only fully achievable ends are worth pursuing. To better understand this, consider two examples.

Adolf Hitler held up the creation of a "perfect" Aryan race of blue-eyed, blond-haired people as an ideal. To characterize Hitler's program as "too idealistic" and to argue that he could never fully achieve his aim, and therefore, he should have been more "realistic" seems to misunderstand the moral situation. The problem was not that the ideal was unattainable but that it was a terrible ideal.

In contrast, in his powerful 1963 speech on the steps of the Lincoln Memorial, Martin Luther King Jr. came to collect on the "promissory note"[7] drafted in the Declaration of Independence. He passionately described his vision for a world in which people of all races and creeds lived together in mutual respect and harmony. This "dream" is clearly and explicitly idealistic. As an ideal, it is *not* fully achievable. This world never has been and likely never will be one of perfect equality. However, just because King's ideal of equality is not fully achievable does not mean it should not be pursued. Would, as Lachs proposes, the proper response be that King's ideal of equality is a "perverse desire to heap infinite obligations on finite individuals"? In pursuing this unattainable ideal of perfect equality, is King "guarantee[ing] moral failure" and "making life miserable"?[8] This interpretation of the moral situation suggests a flawed understanding of the role and nature of moral ideals.

Moral ideals such as the great work of deep sustainability and self-stewardship are not meaningful because they are achievable but because they define success and failure, better and worse. Without moral ideals, making comparative moral judgments becomes arbitrary. Ideals serve as the standards by which to judge the success of

---

7. Martin Luther King Jr., "I Have a Dream" (Lincoln Memorial, Washington, DC, August 28, 1963), in *I Have a Dream: Writings and Speeches That Changed the World*, ed. James M. Washington (San Francisco: Harper SanFrancisco, 1992), 102.

8. Lachs, "Good Enough," 1.

one's actions. To borrow a geometrical example, moral ideals are like asymptotes. Just as an asymptote can infinitely approach but never reach a limit, actions can get closer or farther from an ideal (see fig. 6.1). The Emancipation Proclamation (1863), Women's Suffrage (1920), and the Civil Rights Act (1964) each brought the United States a step closer to achieving the ideal of equality. Racial profiling, extraordinary rendition (the practice of transporting suspected terrorists to countries with lax safeguards against abusive interrogation), and suspension of habeas corpus (the legal procedure preventing governments from holding people without demonstrating cause) each move us farther away.

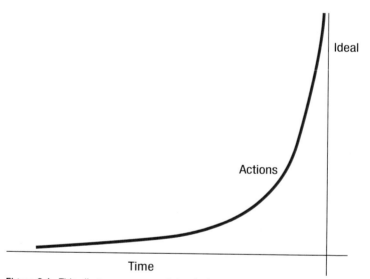

Figure 6.1. This diagram, an asymptote, depicts a characteristic of moral ideals. The vertical axis denotes the ideal and the horizontal axis denotes time. The red line denotes one's actions, which can approach the ideal but, like an asymptote, can never reach the ideal or limit.

A person cannot simply discard moral ideals. One can choose not to explore or examine the basis of one's actions, but actions always occur within an understanding of the good—within a moral framework. Views like Lachs's uphold a standard of "good enough." That is not necessarily a bad thing. Because ideals are inherently unattainable, people can only partially succeed in reaching them.

However, the idea of "good enough" only makes sense in relationship to some good. It is meaningful only insofar as it relates to an ideal. By abandoning the project of defining and defending moral ideals, Lachs loses any basis from which to criticize a given course of action. For example, despite his claim to being "rightly horrified" by "destructive processes" like ethnic cleansing, Lachs has no ultimate basis from which to justify his horror.[9]

Not only does Lachs reject moral ideals as infinite obligations put on finite beings, he criticizes the human tendency to be dissatisfied with anything less than the perfect. He characterizes this refusal to accept the standard of "good enough" as the source of human dissatisfaction and personal misery. But is that the primary source of dissatisfaction? Could one not also trace the source of dissatisfaction to the pursuit of fundamentally unworthy ideals? For instance, defining happiness as the quest for physical pleasure or the acquisition of wealth could set one up for misery and failure. The more pleasure and wealth one has, the more one seems to want. Enough, as Lachs notes, is never good enough.

The Dalai Lama puts this point well when he notes that trying to achieve happiness through the senses is like drinking saltwater to sate one's thirst. The more one drinks, the thirstier one grows.[10] Yet contrary to Lachs's conclusion, the problem does not derive from pursuing an unachievable ideal but rather from pursuing a poor ideal. As the Dalai Lama argues, the situation looks quite different when pursuing an alternate moral ideal. Rather than wealth accumulation, he suggests the moral ideal of *nying je chenmo*, or unconditional love and compassion for all beings.[11] "Of course," the Dalai Lama admits, "even as an ideal, the notion of developing unconditional compassion is daunting. Most people, including myself, must struggle even to reach the point where putting others' interest on a par with our own becomes easy. We should not allow this to put us off, however."[12] The Dalai Lama holds that greater compassion and self-giving results in increased fulfillment and satisfaction. Although

---

9. Ibid., 5.

10. Dalai Lama, *Ethics for the New Millennium* (New York: Riverhead Books, 1999), 52.

11. Ibid., 124–32.

12. Ibid., 130.

the ideal of unconditional love and total compassion for all things remains unachievable, one becomes more deeply satisfied the closer one gets to this ideal.

Philosopher Alfred North Whitehead defines ideals as the "supreme example of consciously formulated ideas acting as a driving force effecting transitions from social state to social state. Such ideas are at once gadflies irritating, and beacons luring, the victims among whom they dwell."[13] The opening lines of Martin Luther King Jr.'s "I Have a Dream" speech beautifully illustrate this dual function:[14]

> Five score years ago, a great American, in whose symbolic shadow we stand today, signed the Emancipation Proclamation. This momentous decree came as a great *beacon light* of hope to millions of Negro slaves who had been seared in the flames of withering injustice. It came as a joyous daybreak to end the long night of their captivity.[15]

The moral ideal of equality offers a "beacon light" luring listeners to a community of justice. However, the same ideal also functions as a "gadfly irritating," chastising all for the failure to live up to its high standard. As King continues,

> But one hundred years later, the Negro still is not free. One hundred years later, the life of the Negro is still sadly crippled by the manacles of segregation and the chains of discrimination. One hundred years later, the Negro lives on a lonely island of poverty in the midst of a vast ocean of material prosperity. One hundred years later, the Negro is still languished in the corners of American society and finds

---

13. Alfred North Whitehead, *Adventures of Ideas* (New York: The Macmillan Company, 1933), 17–18.

14. Though there are doubtless many sources of inspiration for King, it is interesting to note that he did read Whitehead's works closely, and they may have been one of the influences on King's writings. See "Whitehead, Alfred North, *The King Center* (website), *www.thekingcenter.org/archive/theme/4465*. King even quotes Whitehead directly in his 1964 Nobel Peace Prize acceptance speech. Martin Luther King Jr., "The Quest for Peace and Justice," December 11, 1964, Nobelprize.org, *http://bit.ly/1hTXCWf*.

15. King, "I Have a Dream," 102, emphasis added.

himself an exile in his own land. And so we've come here today to dramatize a shameful condition.[16]

Moral ideals are the indispensable driving force behind all progress. They can help create what King calls "creative tension" in his "Letter from a Birmingham Jail."[17] Ideals define direction; they define success and failure; and as Whitehead says, they "nerve all civilized effort."[18]

As Whitehead argues, the "art of life" is not about mere survival but about how to live well and to live better.[19] In this way, the rise and dominance of the mainstream sustainability paradigm provides a good example of what Whitehead calls

> the birth of a methodology [that] is in its essence the discovery of a dodge to live. In its prime [the methodology] satisfies the immediate conditions for the good life. But the good life is unstable: the law of fatigue is inexorable. When any methodology of life has exhausted the novelties within its scope and played upon them up to the incoming of fatigue, one final decision determines the fate of a species. It can stabilize itself, and relapse so as to live; or it can shake itself free, and enter upon the adventure of living better.[20]

Like the methodology Whitehead refers to as a "dodge to live," a shallow sustainability paradigm threatens to reduce morality to mere survival. In a very real sense, he claims that the fate of a species depends on articulating worthier moral ideals. In terms of addressing global climate change, this will likely require humanity to shake itself free of the siren song of unnecessary consumption and perpetual growth and enter the "adventure of living better." The first step

---

16. Ibid., 102.

17. Martin Luther King Jr., "Letter From a Birmingham Jail (1963)," in *I Have a Dream: Writings and Speeches That Changed the World*, ed. James M. Washington (San Francisco: HarperSanFrancisco, 1992), 86.

18. Whitehead, *Adventures of Ideas*, 89.

19. Alfred North Whitehead, *The Function of Reason* (Princeton: Princeton University Press, 1929), 8.

20. Ibid., 18–19.

in this adventure does not entail abandoning ideals but the fallible formulation and dogged pursuit of ideals worthy of life.

While not fully achievable, the ideals embodied in the concepts of great work, deep sustainability, self-stewardship, and voluntary simplicity are nonetheless worth pursuing. The human community must realistically determine what steps will help it achieve a larger share of those ideals; what will move us "up the curve"? Thoughtful individuals who earnestly pursue a life of greater simplicity are no less realistic than those dedicated to the pursuit of ever-greater wealth. In the end this is not a debate between idealism and realism but between competing ideals.

Hypocrisy and the Pursuit of Moral Ideals

The formulation of ideals as asymptotic guides to action creates an unexpected problem. If moral ideals define progress and success but are not fully achievable, then one's actions will fall short of one's stated ideals. There will be a gap between one's stated beliefs and one's actions. It would then seem that anyone who pursues moral ideals is a hypocrite. For instance, in the context of the present discussion, isn't anyone concerned about global climate change a carbon-exhaling hypocrite?

This line of argument is often used to undermine those committed to change based on their ideals. Rather than attack their ideals, critics merely point out that they fall short of them, whether it be voluntary simplicity or developing moral concern for all organisms. There are two problems with this line of reasoning. First, it is logically fallacious, and second, it is morally simplistic.

Hypocrisy as an *Ad Hominem* Attack

Logicians refer to an assault on the character of the agent—as opposed to a critique of the veracity of the argument or statement—an *ad hominem* attack. However, the truth of an argument does not depend on the character or consistency of its advocate. Former vice president Al Gore, for instance, has become a strong advocate of environmental responsibility since his time in office. He produced an award-winning documentary about the dangers of climate change and has staunchly supported global efforts to curb greenhouse gas emissions. However, even if Gore were actually a terrible hypocrite—if he secretly never turns off the lights, drives a Hummer, leaves the water running while he shaves, has an oil derrick in his backyard, strip-mines his property, hunts endangered spotted owls, and eats baby seals—it would in no way affect the truth of his claims about global warming. The *truth* of the message does not depend on the *consistency* of the messenger. Thus even if Gore were the most heinous American polluter, that would have no effect on whether his claims regarding the possible effects of global warming are true (although it would likely have affected his chance at an Oscar).[21]

Moral Finitude

Accusing those pursuing moral ideals of hypocrisy, however, is both logically and morally false. It confuses the difference between moral finitude and moral hypocrisy. Most people would consider the ideals of equality for all, the end of poverty, world peace, and living in harmony with nature worth pursuing. However, these things are not fully achievable; they remain ideals. Despite society's best efforts, there will still be injustice and economic inequality in the world; some will inevitably use aggression to further their ends; and no matter what humans do, we must destroy other living things in order to sustain ourselves. Thus actions in pursuit of an ideal can never be fully consistent. There will always be a gap between what a person can actually do and what he or she claims as an ideal. In the final analysis, there are no clean hands, and moral perfection is illusory. Does this mean that, in the end, hypocrisy is unavoidable for anyone who pursues a moral ideal? Answering this question requires more precisely defining the nature of hypocrisy.

The English word *hypocrisy* is rooted in the ancient Greek word *hypokrisia*, which means playing a part on stage. As the ethicist

---

21. For more on this logical point, see Scott F. Aiken and Robert B. Tallisse, "The Truth about Hypocrisy: Charges of Hypocrisy Can Be Surprisingly Irrelevant and Often Distract Us from More Important Concerns," *Scientific American* (December 3, 2008). See also, Scott F. Aiken, "The Significance of Al Gore's Purported Hypocrisy," *Environmental Ethics* 31 (2009): 111–12.

Tom Regan notes, the contemporary meaning of the word retains this etymology: "Hypocrites are people who play a part. They represent themselves as being better than they are. Although hypocrisy is a form of deception, not all forms of deception involve hypocrisy."[22] This explanation distinguishes deception from hypocrisy, where one is merely "playing a part" or "giving lip service." Failing to live up to one's moral ideals does not, by itself, prove *moral hypocrisy* but rather indicates *moral finitude*. Those who take concrete steps to "move up the curve" toward their moral ideals are *not* hypocrites. They are not merely playing a part or giving lip service. Rather, those who earnestly pursue but fail to fully achieve their moral ideals are morally finite.

TABLE 6.1

Moral Hypocrisy vs. Moral Finitude	
Moral Hypocrisy	**Moral Finitude**
• There is a gap between one's beliefs and one's actions. • One gives only lip-service to one's supposed ideals. • When given the opportunity, one does *not* take steps toward achieving one's stated ideals. • One is morally culpable and blameworthy.	• There is a gap between one's beliefs and one's actions. • This gap morally motivates one to do better. • When given the opportunity, one takes steps toward achieving more of one's stated ideals • One is not morally culpable or blameworthy.

To better understand this distinction between moral hypocrisy and moral finitude, consider the alternative. Take the work of Jane Goodall, who has dedicated her life to saving wild chimpanzees from extinction. She has founded nonprofit organizations such as Roots & Shoots, which encourages young people to make positive change in their community for people, animals, and the environment.

---

22. Tom Regan, "Work, Hypocrisy, and Integrity," in *Defending Animal Rights* (Urbana: University of Illinois Press, 2001), 167.

With tens of thousands of young people in more than 120 countries, the Roots & Shoots network connects youth of all ages who share a desire to create a better world. Young people identify problems in their communities and take action. Through service projects, youth-led campaigns and an interactive website, Roots & Shoots members are making a difference across the globe.[23]

In her effort to spread this message, Goodall flies throughout the world speaking to people about poverty, climate change, and the plight of animals such as chimpanzees. She travels so much that she admits that she has not spent more than two weeks in any one location for years. It does not seem controversial to note that Goodall's goals are very idealistic. A critic who fails to distinguish moral hypocrisy from finitude might criticize Goodall for being hypocritical: she *claims* to be very concerned about anthropogenic climate change, but her world travels leave an enormous carbon footprint. Thus the critic might conclude that Goodall should be ignored because she is a hypocrite. However, is this an accurate moral analysis? What is more morally praiseworthy: traveling the world trying to educate people about the threat of global climate change or

Figure 6.2. Jane Goodall (1934–), an English primatologist, ethologist, and activist, discovered that chimpanzees in the wild create and use simple tools. Today she advocates on behalf of chimpanzees and the environment, travelling nearly 300 days a year to do this work.

© EdStock/Shutterstock.com

---

23. The Jane Goodall Institute, "Roots and Shoots," *www.janegoodall.org /jobs-united-states/co-environmental-service-learning-contractor.*

spending her life in a tent in the jungles of Gombe studying the chimps she loves so much?

Though living in the jungle would have a much smaller ecological footprint, ending her global advocacy would mean that fewer people would understand and address the challenge of anthropogenic climate change. Therefore, if the achievement of more or less of one's moral ideals is the standard of judgment, abandoning her advocacy work would *not* be more morally defensible because it would move her farther from achieving her moral ideals. This illustrates how identifying hypocrisy is not as simple as comparing actions with stated beliefs. The question is whether one merely plays the part or, when given the opportunity, attempts to realize a greater share of his or her moral ideals. Goodall dedicates her most valuable possessions—her time and energy—to convince others to take this issue seriously. In this way, Goodall is not a hypocrite. She is morally finite. In fact, it would be *more* morally unfortunate if Goodall returned to the jungle to minimize her carbon impact. Society needs messengers and prophets; it needs catalysts. Those who pursue moral ideals will always have a gap between their actions and beliefs. The mistake is not in *pursuing* ideals but in believing that only fully achievable ends are worth pursuing.

Table 6.1 summarizes the important distinctions between moral finitude and hypocrisy, which raises the more important question: what can individuals do to realize a greater share of their moral ideals? This is the true work of morality. In the end, the debate over being realistic or idealistic presents a false dilemma. Realistically, one can only bring about desirable states in the world through the concrete pursuit of worthy moral ideals. As the Dalai Lama puts it, "Ideals are the engine of progress. To ignore this and say merely that we need to be 'realistic' in politics is severely mistaken."[24] *The only truly realistic actions are those in service of worthwhile ideals.* The question is not whether ideals are achievable, for no true ideal is. Rather, one should ask:

1. What are my moral ideals?
2. Are they worth pursuing?

---

24. Dalai Lama, *Ethics for the New Millennium*, 197.

3. If they are worth pursuing, what do they require of me here and now?

Recognizing the difference between moral finitude and hypocrisy helps to put the focus on what is most important, namely, evaluating whether one's actions move one closer or farther away from realizing one's moral ideals. It is this question, not the question of hypocrisy, that is most important. That is, moral agents should be judged not on the mere *consistency* of their beliefs and actions but on the *efficacy* of their actions relative to their ideals. The issue then is not whether a person has ideals, but whether he or she has the courage to declare, scrutinize, and pursue them.

The first step toward taking up the great work to make a better world is not the abandonment of ideals but the fallible formulation and dogged pursuit of ideals worthy of one's life.

Having opened this volume with a passage from Thomas Berry, a matching bookend is appropriate in conclusion:

> We are now experiencing a moment of significance far beyond what any of us can imagine. What can be said is that the foundations of a new historical period, the Ecozoic Era, have been established in every realm of human affairs. The mythic vision has been set into place. The distorted dream of an industrial technological paradise is being replaced by the more viable dream of a mutually enhancing human presence within an ever-renewing organic-based Earth community. The dream drives the action. In the larger cultural context the dream becomes the myth that both guides and drives the action.[25]

For Further Exploration

1. Reflect on an instance when you called someone a hypocrite or you were called a hypocrite. Was this an instance of an *ad hominem* attack? Why or why not? In your own life, have you

---

25. Berry, *The Great Work*, 201.

noticed a difference between being morally finite and being a hypocrite?

2. Reflect on some of your most deeply held moral ideals. What practical actions could you take that would move you closer to achieving a larger share of those ideals? Does the fact that moral ideals cannot be fully achieved make them less worth pursuing? Why or why not?

Additional Resources

Aiken, Scott F. "The Significance of Al Gore's Purported Hypocrisy." *Environmental Ethics* 31 (2009): 111–12.

Aiken, Scott F., and Robert B. Tallisse. "The Truth about Hypocrisy: Charges of Hypocrisy Can Be Surprisingly Irrelevant and Often Distract Us from More Important Concerns." *Scientific American* (December 3, 2008).

Regan, Tom. "Work, Hypocrisy, and Integrity." In *Defending Animal Rights*, 164–75 (Urbana: University of Illinois Press, 2001).

Appendix

Eating Animals on a Warming Planet: A Case Study

To ask the biggest questions, we can start with the most personal—what do we eat? What we eat is within our control, yet the act ties us to the economic, political, and ecological order of our whole planet. Even an apparently small change—consciously choosing a diet that is good both for our bodies and for the Earth—can lead to a series of choices that transform our whole lives.[1]

—Frances Moore Lappé, *Diet for a Small Planet*

When confronted by the reality of a changing climate, many rightly wonder what they might do in their own life to address this challenge. If the most severe effects of anthropogenic climate change are to be mitigated, people and nations across the world will not only need to adopt more sustainable practices but will likely need to change deeply held attitudes and habits. Confronting this difficult reality can be daunting, even for those who might want to take up this great work.

College students often find this realization particularly difficult because they feel that they either have little control over or insufficient resources to change the largest contributors to their carbon footprint. Students often are unable to change how their residence is heated and cooled, whether there is sufficient insulation, how often

---

1. Francis Moore Lappé, *Diet for a Small Planet* (New York: Ballantine Books, [1971] 1991), 8.

they travel to see family or to participate in sports, or whether their home appliances are efficient.

However, one of the practices over which most adults, including college students, have considerable control is over the food they eat. Perhaps surprisingly, it turns out that what we eat can play a significant role in contributing to anthropogenic climate change. Often analyses of global warming omit the fact that the food people eat contributes more to global climate change than what they drive or the energy they use. Worldwide, greenhouse gas (GHG) emissions from agriculture exceed both power generation[2] and transportation,[3] contributing as much as one-third of all emissions.[4] Given more time and space, it would be instructive to engage in a study of the climate impact of various food practices, such as the industrial processing of food products, local versus global food production models, and organic versus industrial growing techniques. For instance, if one has to choose between either locally grown food or organically grown food, but cannot have both, which ought one chose and why? These and many other questions are important to ask. This study will focus on food practices related to the production of animals for food.

This focus on the climate impact of global livestock production is appropriate in part because the largest share of agriculture-related GHG emissions (14.5%) come from the raising of animals for their meat.[5] Indeed, it turns out that meat consumption is *more* responsible for global climate change than what we drive or how we heat our

---

2. Anthony J. McMichael et al., "Energy and Health 5: Food, Livestock Production, Energy, Climate Change, and Health," *The Lancet* 370 (2007): 1259.

3. Henning Steinfeld et al., *Livestock's Long Shadow: Environmental Issues and Options* (Rome: Food and Agriculture Organization, 2006), xxi; Nathan Pelletier and Peter Tyedmers, "Forecasting Potential Global Environmental Costs of Livestock Production 2000–2050," *Proceedings of the National Academy of Science* 107, no. 43 (October 26, 2010): 2.

4. Jessica Bellarby et al., "Evaluating the Environmental Impact of Various Dietary Patterns Combined with Different Forms of Production Systems," *European Journal of Clinical Nutrition* 61 (2008): 5. Bellarby writes, "The total global contribution of agriculture, considering all direct and indirect emissions, is . . . between 17 and 32% of all global human-induced GHG emissions, including land use change" (5).

5. Food and Agriculture Organization (FAO), *Tackling Climate Change through Livestock: A Global Assessment of Emissions and Mitigation Opportunities* (Rome: FAO, 2013), xii.

homes.[6] Thus given the large role it plays and given that most adults have immediate and on-going control over whether to eat meat or not, examining the ethics of eating meat in a world transformed by global warming may be a helpful case study. Although this study will focus on the production of animals, it provides a roadmap for how one might examine other cases.

The analysis will proceed in two parts. Before making any moral judgments, it is important to have a sense of the morally relevant facts related to the particular case. Thus the first part examines the extent of the role of global livestock production in contributing to global climate change. Given this context, the second part then considers both the strengths and weakness of three possible ways of mitigating the impact of meat-related emissions: (1) improving the efficiency of industrial methods, (2) shifting away from intensive, industrial methods toward extensive, pasture-based methods, or (3) shifting away from the consumption of animals, whether partially or entirely.

Meat Production's Role in Climate Change

The livestock sector is often omitted or ignored in discussions of global climate change because it contributes a relatively small

---

6. According to the FAO, "With rising temperatures, rising sea levels, melting ice-caps and glaciers, shifting ocean current and weather patterns, climate change is the most serious challenge facing the human race. The livestock sector is a major player, responsible for 18 percent of greenhouse gas emissions measured in CO_2 equivalent. This is a higher share than transport." Steinfeld et al., *Livestock's Long Shadow*, xxi. Other scholars have rightly noted that the FAO's comparison of the livestock and transportation sectors is potentially misleading because it is "based on inappropriate or inaccurate scaling of predictions." Maurice E. Pitesky, Kimberly R. Stackhouse, and Frank M. Miltloehner, "Cleaning the Air: Livestock's Contribution to Climate Change," in *Advances in Agronomy*, vol. 103, ed. Donald Sparks (Burlington: Academic Press, 2009), 33. Thus these scholars do *not* dispute that livestock production accounts for 18% of global greenhouse gas emissions. Rather, their claim is first that the FAO's *comparison* of the livestock and transportation sectors is misleading because, whereas both direct and indirect emissions are included for the livestock sector, only direct emissions are counted for the transportation sector. Secondly, they note that while it is true that the livestock sector has a larger footprint than transportation in many developing nations, it is not true of the United States (and most developed nations) where livestock account for only 2.8% of emissions (4). Thus these scholars rightly note that a more precise formulation would be to say that "agriculture is considered the largest source of anthropogenic CH_4 and N_2O at the global, national, and state level, . . . while transport is considered the largest anthropogenic source of CO_2 production" (11).

portion of direct global carbon dioxide (CO_2) emissions (9%), primarily from the burning of biomass (deforestation) to create feed crops or pasture.[7] However, a closer analysis reveals meat production has a much larger role in the emission of methane, a potent heat-trapping gas.

While CO_2 concentrations in the atmosphere have increased by more than one-third over preindustrial levels, methane concentrations have more than doubled in the last two centuries.[8] Methane is formed through anaerobic breakdown of organic matter. Thus there are natural sources of methane, the most important of which are wetlands and termite mounds. The major anthropogenic sources are coal mining, leakage from natural gas pipelines and oil wells, rice paddies, biomass burning (burning of wood and peat), and most important for present purposes, waste treatment (manure) and enteric fermentation (bovine flatulence).[9] Though still present in the atmosphere in far smaller amounts than CO_2—1.9 parts per million (ppm) vs. 400 ppm—methane plays a disproportionate role in global warming, contributing 21% of all anthropogenic warming[10] because of differences in the molecular properties of atmospheric methane.

Unlike CO_2, which is gradually absorbed by land biota or the ocean,[11] methane chemically breaks down in the atmosphere, lasting an average of only 12 years.[12] This relatively short life cycle is offset

---

7. The analysis in this appendix is an abbreviated version of Brian G. Henning, "Standing in Livestock's 'Long Shadow': The Ethics of Eating Meat on a Small Planet," *Ethics & the Environment* 16, no. 2 (2011): 63–94.

8. John Houghton, *Global Warming: The Complete Briefing*, 4th ed. (Cambridge: Cambridge University Press, 2009), 20, 50.

9. Ibid., 50. For a list of methane emission by source, see p. 53, table 32.

10. Ibid., 35.

11. Although the shorthand of one century is often used for the lifetime of carbon in the atmosphere, the actual life cycle is more complicated because reservoirs "turn over" at a wide range of timescales, "which range from less than a year to decades (for exchange with the top layers of the ocean and the land biosphere) to millennia (for exchange with the deep ocean or long-lived soil pools)" (ibid.).

12. Houghton writes, "The main process for the removal of methane from the atmosphere is through chemical destruction. It reacts with hydroxyl (OH) radicals, which are present in the atmosphere because of processes involving sunlight, oxygen, ozone, and water vapour. The average lifetime of methane in the atmosphere is determined by the rate of this loss process. At about 12 years, it is much shorter than the lifetime of carbon dioxide" (ibid., 50).

by the fact that methane is far more potent at trapping heat than CO_2 is. Indeed, molecule-for-molecule, methane traps twenty-five times as much heat as CO_2 does.[13] Taking this differing global warming potential into account, scientists can calculate the overall footprint of livestock production in terms of CO_2 equivalent (CO_2e). According to one study, "to produce 1 kg (2.2 pounds) of beef in a US feedlot requires the equivalent of 14.8 kg (32.6 pounds) of CO_2. As a comparison, 1 gallon (3.8 liters) of gasoline emits approximately 2.4 kg (5.3 pounds) of CO_2. Producing 1 kg of beef thus has a similar impact on the environment as 6.2 gallons (23.5 L) of gasoline, or driving 160 miles (257 km) in the average American mid-size car."[14] Overall, factoring in both direct and indirect emissions and the differences in life cycle and potency of different gases, the livestock sector is responsible for approximately 15% of all GHG emissions worldwide.[15]

The effect of even the relatively small amount of warming 0.8°C (1.44°F) in the twentieth century is already being felt. As chapters 1 and 2 examined, in coming decades these changes will accelerate with the rising temperature. Though there will be regional winners and losers, generally those least responsible for causing the heat-trapping gases (developing nations and nature) are expected to be most severely affected by the changing climate. These effects include melting icecaps and glaciers, rising sea levels, shifting weather patterns, more intense storms, drought, desertification, species extinction, salinization of freshwater, spread of infectious disease, and millions of environmental refugees.

The urgency of this realization becomes even more apparent when considered in light of the rapidly accelerating rate of meat consumption, which is expected to more than double by 2050 from the 1990 level of 229 million tons (208 million metric tons)

---

13. See chapter 2, table 2.1 for more on GHG concentrations and table 2.2 for more on the comparative global warming potential of each GHG.

14. Nathan Fiala, "Meeting the Demand: An Estimation of Potential Future Greenhouse Gas Emissions from Meat Production," *Ecological Economics* 67 (2008): 413.

15. Steinfeld et al., *Livestock's Long Shadow*, xxi; Brian Halweil, "Meat Production Continues to Rise," *Worldwatch Institute* (August 20, 2008), 2, *www.worldwatch.org/node/5443/*; and Pelletier and Tyedmers, "Forcasting," 2, all suggested livestock contributes 18% of global anthropogenic GHG emissions. The more recent report (FAO, *Tackling Climate Change through Livestock*) puts livestock's contribution at 14.5%.

per year to 465 million tons (422 million metric tons).[16] As the United Nations' Food and Agriculture Organization (FAO) notes, the "environmental impact per unit of livestock" must be halved just to maintain the current level of environmental damage, which is already environmentally unsustainable.[17]

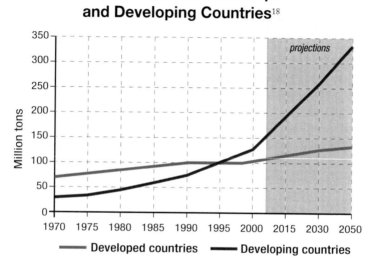

Figure A.1. This graph presents the UN Food and Agriculture Organization's data on actual meat production through 2006 and projections for meat production through 2050. Notice the dramatic increase projected for developing nations. As of 2014, the projections remain accurate.

Three Scenarios for Reducing the Climate Impact of Livestock

Given its characteristically guarded manner, the FAO is surprisingly direct: "Better policies in the livestock sector are an environmental

---

16. Steinfeld et al., *Livestock's Long Shadow*, xx. In a subsequent report, the FAO argues that "growth in animal-source foods will be particularly strong; the demand for meat and milk in 2050 is projected to grow by 73 and 58 percent, respectively, from their levels in 2010." FAO, *Tackling Climate Change through Livestock*, 1.

17. Steinfeld et al., *Livestock's Long Shadow*, xx.

18. The data represented in this graph is from Ibid., 15.

requirement, and a social and health necessity."[19] Given that livestock's "contribution to environmental problems is on a massive scale . . . its potential contribution to their solution is equally large. The impact is so significant that it needs to be addressed with urgency. Major reductions in impact could be achieved at reasonable cost."[20] Given this conclusion, this section will examine three possible responses: (1) greater efficiency of meat production, (2) transition back to grass-fed and free-range meat production, and (3) transition toward reduced meat consumption, vegetarianism, or veganism. Along the way, both the strengths and weaknesses of each response will be considered.

Efficiency, Technology, and the Market

Because meat production is a large source of the gases contributing to climate change, the FAO suggests that livestock production methods need to be made more efficient. They suggest that policymakers and industry leaders follow specific measures to mitigate the environmental impact of livestock production.[21]

- Agricultural **subsidies**: Governments should commit to the gradual elimination of "often perverse subsidies," which too often "encourage livestock producers to engage in environmentally damaging activities."[22]
- Manure: Research and implementation of integrated manure management practices should be accelerated, including biogas digestion and methane-capturing systems. This technology has the benefit of capturing heat-trapping methane as an energy source, reducing water pollution, and creating high-quality fertilizer that can return nutrients to the soil.[23]

---

19. Ibid., 4.

20. Ibid., xx.

21. This is not a complete list of the FAO's recommendations. See Henning, "Standing in Livestock's 'Long Shadow'" or Steinfeld et al., *Livestock's Long Shadow* for a more complete analysis.

22. Steinfeld et al., *Livestock's Long Shadow*, xxiii–xxiv.

23. Ibid., 279. The immediate viability of manure management systems is questioned by Fiala, who claims that "this technology is a long way from being used in the US and Europe, let alone the rest of the world; this is not likely to be a solution in the near future." Fiala, "Meeting the Demand," 418.

- Concentrated animal feeding operations (CAFOs): Developing nations should follow the path of developed nations and *accelerate* the transition to intensive, industrial livestock production to increase resource efficiency and decrease environmental damage per unit of livestock.[24]

From the perspective of ethicists and activists concerned with animal welfare, the FAO's most controversial recommendation is likely that nations should *hasten* the transition to CAFOs, also known as factory farms. However, the FAO claims that the environmental problems caused by industrial livestock production are not from their "large scale" or "production intensity" but from their "geographical location and concentration."[25] For instance, the FAO argues that raising animals in CAFOs rather than pasture-based methods will *decrease* deforestation motivated by the creation of pasture or feedstock, thereby reducing a major source of GHG emissions caused by the livestock sector.[26]

With the exception of controversial CAFOs, many scholars agree with the FAO's suggested changes to livestock production methods. However, some question whether these changes are *sufficient* to mitigate livestock production's high cost to the environment. As Nathan Pelletier and Peter Tyedmers of the Dalhousie University School for Resource and Environmental Studies in Halifax, Nova Scotia, conclude in their analysis of the FAO report: "Given the magnitude of necessary efficiency gains, it would appear highly unlikely that technological improvements alone will be sufficient to achieve the objective of maintaining the proportional contribution of the livestock sector to cumulative anthropogenic contributions to these issues."[27] They conclude that, even if all of the FAO's recommended measures were implemented, meat production practices would remain unsustainable. As Pelletier and Tyedmers put it, there is a "profound disconnect between the anticipated scale of potential

---

24. Steinfeld et al., *Livestock's Long Shadow*, 278.

25. Ibid.

26. The FAO contends, "Expansion of livestock production is a key factor in deforestation, especially in Latin America where the greatest amount of deforestation is occurring—70 percent of previous forested land in the Amazon is occupied by pastures, and feedcrops cover a large part of the remainder" (ibid., xxi).

27. Pelletier and Tyedmers, "Forecasting," 3.

environmental impacts associated with projected livestock production levels and the most optimistic mitigations strategies relative to these current, published estimates of sustainable biocapacity."[28]

In focusing exclusively on *reforming* livestock production methods and refusing also to recommend explicitly the *reduction* of meat consumption, the concern is that the FAO's report gives the false impression that current meat consumption practices can indefinitely continue, if only methods were made more efficient.[29] The concern is that these market-based technical fixes would do too little to solve the problem. Indeed, in a telling passage, the FAO seems to recognize this, noting that "by applying scientific knowledge and technological capability" we can at best "offset" some of the damage. "Meanwhile, the vast legacy of damage leaves future generations with a debt."[30] Recognizing that even reformed industrial livestock production methods are likely insufficient, some are calling for more dramatic changes to the way animals are raised.

Let Them Eat Grass

A raft of largely popular books decrying the industrialization of food production has reached a new high-water mark, led most vocally and eloquently by the journalist Michael Pollan.[31] Unlike the philosophers and activists of an earlier generation who, inspired by the work of Peter Singer and Tom Regan, fought against industrial farming

---

28. Ibid.

29. In its otherwise comprehensive and detailed analysis, the FAO makes only one brief reference to the role of meat consumption. "While not being addressed in this assessment, it may well be argued that environmental damage by livestock may be significantly reduced by lowering excessive consumption of livestock products among wealthy people." Steinfeld et al., *Livestock's Long Shadow,* 269.

30. Ibid., 5.

31. See, for instance, Eric Schlosser, *Fast Food Nation* (New York: Houghton Mifflin, 2001); Eric Schlosser and Charles Wilson, *Chew on This: Everything You Don't Want to Know about Fast Food* (New York: Houghton Mifflin, 2006); Michael Pollan, *The Omnivore's Dilemma: A Natural History of Four Meals* (New York: Penguin, 2007); Michael Pollan, *In Defense of Food: An Eater's Manifesto* (New York: Penguin, 2009); Barbara Kingsolver, *Animal, Vegetable, Miracle* (New York: HarperCollins, 2007); Carlo Petrini, *Slow Food Nation* (New York: Rizzoli Ex Libris, 2007); Jonathan Safran Foer, *Eating Animals* (New York: Little, Brown, 2009); Simon Fairlie, *Meat: A Benign Extravagance* (White River Junction, VT: Chelsea Green Publishing, 2010).

because of the excessive suffering caused to animals, this "new agrarian farming movement" is focused more on the human and environmental costs of industrialized food production.[32] Though the movement is diverse, it is largely characterized by a return to more "natural" methods of producing food and raising animals, including local, organic produce and free-range animals. Thus there is a hue and cry for a movement away from CAFOs, not necessarily because of the pain and suffering that they undeniably cause to the animals, but because of the human and environmental damage they inflict. While a complete analysis of the new agrarian movement is not possible here, it is important to consider whether and how a move from *intensive* factory farming to *extensive* pasture-based methods would address some of the human and environmental damages currently caused by livestock production.

First, proponents of this view note that new agrarian methods would dramatically improve the lives of livestock. As philosophers and animal activists have rightly noted for decades, intensive factory farming methods (especially in the United States) are unimaginably cruel. There is little dispute among those who study the issue that most of the animals raised in CAFOs lead short lives of intense suffering, particularly chickens and pigs. "The crucial moral difference," Pollan rightly notes, "between a CAFO and a good farm is that the CAFO systematically deprives the animals in it of their 'characteristic form of life.'"[33] Animals should be returned, Pollan argues, to their rightful evolutionary role as members of a complex farming community symbiotically related in complex webs of interdependence.[34]

Second, the new agrarians argue that the elimination of CAFOs would not only be good for the animals themselves, it would likely result in significant reductions in livestock-related emissions because

---

32. I will use the phrase "new agrarian movement" to refer to the loose collection of popular writers and scholars who seek to move society away from industrial food production. This phrase is inspired by the book series created by the University Press of Kentucky, Culture of the Land: A Series in the New Agrarianism. See *www.kentuckypress.com/live/series_detail.php?seriesID=CULL*. My thanks to Lee McBride for bringing this series to my attention.

33. Pollan, *Omnivore's Dilemma*, 321.

34. On the symbiosis between livestock and humans, see ibid.

its methods require *much* smaller herds and flocks. Significant reductions in the number of animals raised worldwide would have a relatively immediate positive effect on global climate change, especially compared to other possible changes, such as lower-carbon forms of energy production or transportation. Since a significant portion of livestock-related emissions are in the form of methane, which is twenty-five times more potent in trapping heat than CO_2, removing one molecule of methane is equivalent to removing twenty-five molecules of CO_2. Further, unlike a molecule of CO_2, which on average remains in the atmosphere for a century, methane has a lifetime of little more than a decade (twelve years).[35] Thus in raising far fewer animals, new agrarian methods would likely decrease meat-related GHG emissions significantly, though there are no known studies that have tried to model this precisely.

Finally, the new agrarians argue that its methods would also be good for human health. The combination of smaller herds and flocks and the proposed elimination of agricultural subsidies would dramatically increase the price of meat and other industrially processed foods. This decrease in supply and increase in price of meat would likely result in a reduction in consumption, which would likely have significant benefits for human health. As the British medical journal *The Lancet* found in its study, a "substantial contraction" in meat consumption in developed nations should benefit human health "mainly by reducing the risk of ischaemic heart disease . . . , obesity, colorectal cancer, and, perhaps, some other cancers."[36] In this way, proponents of the new agrarian movement argue, meat would remain a part of the human diet, but it would play a noticeably smaller role. Thus, in sum, the new agrarian movement wants far more dramatic changes in livestock production methods than those advocated by the United Nations but does not go so far as to argue explicitly that humans should moderate or eliminate meat from their diet.

This return to a more "traditional diet" was first championed by Frances Moore Lappé, the Rachel Carson of the food movement.[37]

---

35. See chapter 2 for a discussion of global warming potentials.

36. McMichael et al., "Energy and Health," 1254.

37. Lappé, *Diet for a Small Planet*, 13.

Animal flesh has been part of the diet of *Homo sapiens* for millions of years, but until recently it has always played a minor role. This evolutionary perspective on meat eating is also at the heart of Pollan's discussion in his acclaimed *The Omnivore's Dilemma*. Pollan takes issue with animal welfare advocates who equate the domestication and raising of animals with "exploitation" or "slavery," arguing that this portrays a fundamental misunderstanding of the relationship between humans and livestock. "Domestication is an evolutionary, rather than a political, development," Pollan writes. "It is certainly not a regime humans somehow imposed on animals some ten thousand years ago."[38] Rather, Pollan argues, the raising of animals for food and labor is an instance of human predation, and as such it is an instance of "mutualism or symbiosis between species."[39] He suggests that humans should see the raising and consuming of animals not as a regrettable moral failing but as an ecologically vital part of our evolutionary heritage. "Indeed," Pollan argues, "it is doubtful you can build a genuinely sustainable agriculture without animals to cycle nutrients and support local food production. If our concern is for the health of nature—rather than, say, the internal consistency of our moral code or the condition of our souls—then eating animals may be the most ethical thing to do."[40] Thus, overall, advocates of the new agrarian movement argue that compared to the dominant industrial model, the organic, pasture-based methods are better for the animals raised, for the humans who eat them, and for our shared natural environment.

Yet some scholars have questioned whether pointing, as Pollan and Lappé do, to the evolutionary basis of meat consumption is a sufficient moral justification of continuing the practice. Explaining the *biological genesis* of a practice is not yet to have given a *moral justification* for the practice. Indeed, Pollan himself makes this point. "Do you really want to base your moral code on the natural order? Murder and rape are natural, too. Besides, we can choose: humans don't need to kill other creatures in order to survive; carnivorous animals do."[41]

---

38. Pollan, *Omnivore's Dilemma*, 320.

39. Ibid.

40. Ibid., 327.

41. Ibid., 320.

Given that humans don't *need* to kill and consume other animals in order to survive or even thrive,[42] the *choice* to do so requires moral justification, says Pollan. Beyond the evolutionary argument, the moral weight of the argument for continuing to eat animals would seem to rest on the claim that truly sustainable agriculture requires the use of livestock to complete the nutrient cycle. Yet some scholars remain unconvinced.

Vasile Stănescu, a Stanford University doctoral student focusing on animal ethics and the environment, contends that the underlying narrative of the new agrarianism "is simply factually untrue."[43] Given the world's current and projected rate of meat consumption, he argues that it is not physically possible to raise sufficient livestock via pasture-based methods: "Locally based meat, regardless of its level of popularity, can never constitute more than either a rare and occasional novelty item, or food choices for only a few privileged customers, since there simply is not enough arable land left in the entire world to raise large quantities of pasture-fed animals necessary to meet the world's meat consumption."[44] Thus Stănescu is questioning whether the new agrarianism is misleading because it gives (wealthy) consumers in the developed world the impression that they can basically continue their current rate of meat consumption as long as they pay a premium for grass-fed or pasture-raised animals. This seems to be the key issue: is it really *possible* to feed sustainably the present and projected human population on a diet based significantly on the consumption of animals without significantly contributing to anthropogenic climate change? Some scholars contend that the change in methods suggested by the FAO and even the new agrarianism are insufficient. They suggest that, given the scale

---

42. This is confirmed by the American Dietetic Association: "The results of an evidenced based review showed that a vegetarian diet is associated with a lower risk of death from ischemic heart disease. Vegetarians also appear to have lower low-density lipoprotein cholesterol levels, lower blood pressure, and lower rates of hypertension and type 2 diabetes than nonvegetarians. Furthermore, vegetarians tend to have a lower body mass index and lower overall cancer rates." "Position of the American Dietetic Association: Vegetarian Diets," *Journal of the American Dietetic Association* 109, no. 7 (2009), 1266.

43. Vasile Stănescu, "'Green' Eggs and Ham? The Myth of Sustainable Meat and the Danger of the Local," *Journal for Critical Animal Studies* 8 (2010): 12.

44. Ibid., 14–15.

of the ecological challenges we have created and the projected size of the human community, meat consumption needs to be dramatically reduced, if not eliminated.

Choosing to Eat Less Meat

What diet is most desirable in a world with 7 to 10 billion humans? In their scientific study of the FAO's report, researchers Pelletier and Tyedmers attempt to quantify the likely environmental impacts that diet will have in 2050. Specifically, they examine three different dietary scenarios for meeting the US Department of Agriculture (USDA) recommendations for protein consumption.[45] The FAO projection scenario represents the status quo baseline of projected increases in animal product consumption, which is expected to increase 73% over 2010 levels by 2050.[46] In the "substitution scenario," Pelletier and Tyedmers consider the environmental impact of replacing less efficient ruminant products (cows, sheep, goats, milk) with monogastic products (chickens, turkeys, eggs). Finally, Pelletier and Tyedmers consider the anticipated environmental impact of a "soy protein scenario," in which the recommended daily allowance (RDA) of protein is derived entirely from soy protein sources (vegan diet).

This study then compares each of these scenarios against recent estimates of "environmental boundary conditions" for sustainable GHG emissions, reactive nitrogen mobilization,[47] and anthropogenic biomass appropriation (the quantity of living matter appropriated for human use). These boundary conditions are defined as "biophysical limits which define a safe operating space for economic activities at

---

45. Pelletier and Tyedmers, "Forecasting," 3.

46. FAO, *Tackling Climate Change through Livestock*, 1.

47. They explain this term in the following way: "Nitrogen is essential to all life forms and is also the most abundant element in the Earth's atmosphere. Atmospheric N, however, exists in a stable form (N_2) inaccessible to most organisms until fixed in a reactive form (N-). The supply of reactive nitrogen plays a pivotal role in controlling the productivity, carbon storage, and species composition of ecosystems. . . . Alteration of the nitrogen cycle has numerous consequences, including increased radiative forcing [i.e., climate change], photochemical smog and acid deposition, and productivity increases leading to ecosystem simplification and biodiversity loss." Pelletier and Tyedmers, "Forecasting," 1.

a global scale."[48] Pelletier and Tyedmers's study provides a helpful model for evaluating the sustainability of human activity with regard to these three critical areas. *All* human activity—not only food production but also energy production, manufacturing, transportation—must fall within these "environmental boundary conditions" for humanity to avert "irreversible ecological change."[49]

While recognizing that their models still embody "considerable uncertainty," Pelletier and Tyedmers find that "by 2050, the livestock sector alone may either occupy the majority of, or considerably overshoot, current best estimates of humanity's safe operating space in each of these domains."[50] Specifically, they found that by 2050, to meet FAO projected livestock demand (FAO scenario), livestock production will require 70% of the sustainable boundary conditions for GHG emissions, 88% of sustainable biomass appropriation, and 294% of sustainable reactive nitrogen mobilization.[51] Thus according to their conservative estimates, if humans consume animal-sourced proteins at the rates projected by the FAO, *livestock production alone* will consume the majority of or exceed entirely the sustainable boundary conditions in these three critical areas.

Note that, since they are limited to *direct* GHG emissions and *direct* appropriation of biomass, these figures are, if anything, likely to be overly conservative. If *indirect* emissions and biomass appropriations are included, such as the effects of land-use conversion, then it is likely that the sustainable boundary conditions for both GHG emissions and biomass appropriation would also be exceeded. That

---

48. Ibid., 1–2.

49. Ibid., 3.

50. Ibid., 2. The researchers admit the speculative nature of their models but also note the conservative nature of the presuppositions made. "Modeling the future is fraught with uncertainties, and we would be remiss to present our estimates as definitive. We have endeavored to err on the side of caution in developing what we believe to be conservative forecasts of some of the potential future environmental impacts of livestock production. For example, it would be impressive, indeed, were all livestock production globally to achieve resource efficiencies comparable to those reported for the least impactful contemporary systems in industrialized countries, effectively reducing global impacts per unit protein produced by 35 percent in 2050 relative to 2000—as we have assumed here" (ibid).

51. Ibid.

is, it is possible that livestock production alone could use the entirety of the annual allowable emissions to maintain a stable climate.[52]

What if, instead of relying on ruminant sources of protein (beef, sheep, goat, and milk), humans derived their protein from more efficient, monogastric sources (chicken, turkey, and eggs) as in the substitution scenario?[53] According to their analysis, the "substitution scenario" would only yield an aggregate reduction in environmental impacts of 5–13% relative to the FAO projection scenario, casting doubt on the sustainability of a diet of mainly monogastric animals.[54] Thus while eating chicken instead of beef, or turkey instead of lamb would reduce the ecological impact of livestock, on a planet with 9 billion people it would not be sufficient to make this scenario sustainable.

What if (theoretically) all of the projected 9 billion humans in 2050 instead obtained their recommended daily intake of protein from plant (in this case soybean) sources, as in the "soy protein scenario"? Creating the 457,986 tons (415,478 metric tons) of soybeans[55] necessary to feed the projected 9 billion humans would have a considerable impact on the environment. However, relative to the FAO scenario for 2050, it would represent a 98% reduction of GHG emissions, a 94%

---

52. Nathan Pelletier and Peter Tyedmers, "Forecasting Potential Global Environmental Costs of Livestock Production 2000-2050: Supporting Information," *Proceedings of the National Academy of Science* 107, no. 43 (October 26, 2010), 3. In modeling the likely direct emissions and biomass appropriation, Pelletier and Tyedmers provide an important response to the widely touted work of Pitesky, Stackhouse, and Mitloehner, which takes issue with several of the FAO's conclusions. Notice also that, according to Pelletier and Tyedmers's model, the FAO is mistaken in claiming that increasing the use of CAFOs in developing nations would make production sustainable relative to GHG emissions. Even the most efficient livestock production methods would use an unsustainable portion of the environmental boundary conditions for CO_2 emissions, nitrogen mobilization, and especially, biomass appropriation.

53. This is in fact the suggestion of the article responding to Pelletier and Tyedmers by Henning Steinfeld and Pierre Gerber, "Livestock Production and the Global Environment: Consume Less or Produce Better?" *Proceedings of the National Academy of Science* 107, no. 43 (October 26, 2010), 18237–38.

54. According to Pelletier and Tyedmers, if people consumed poultry products instead of ruminants, "anticipated marginal CO_2-e emissions would rise by 22 percent and biomass appropriation would increase by 15 percent relative to year 2000 levels. . . . However, relative to the FAO projections scenario, substituting poultry for marginal ruminant production would reduce GHG emissions by only 13 percent, biomass appropriation by 5 percent, and reactive nitrogen mobilization by 8 percent." Pelletier and Tyedmers, "Supporting Information," 3.

55. Ibid.

reduction in biomass appropriation, and a 32% reduction in reactive nitrogen mobilization. Thus the entire human population could, in principle, meet its protein needs from plant sources and only contribute 1.1% of sustainable GHG emissions, 6% of sustainable biomass appropriation, and 69% of sustainable reactive nitrogen mobilization.[56] According to this analysis, a plant-based diet is the most sustainable diet in that it offers the least destructive way of obtaining the necessary protein and calories.[57]

Thus proponents of this view argue that, even under the most optimistic scenarios for technological improvements in livestock efficiency, 9 billion humans cannot continue to eat animals at the current and projected rates and avoid catastrophic environmental harms. "As the human species runs the final course of rapid population growth before beginning to level off midcentury," Pelletier and Tyedmers write, "reining in the global livestock sector should be considered a key leverage point for averting irreversible ecological change and moving humanity toward a safe and sustainable operating space."[58] If this analysis is correct, it would seem that humans will not only need to reduce the ecological impact of the animals they raise for food but also reduce the *level* of consumption. According to this view, to successfully address climate change, humans need to reduce meat consumption, perhaps rather dramatically. This is in fact the conclusion of the Chair of the United Nations Intergovernmental Panel on Climate Change (IPCC), Dr. Rajendra Pachauri, an Indian economist. "In terms of immediacy of action and the feasibility of bringing about reductions in a short period of time, it clearly is the most attractive opportunity. . . . Give up meat for one day [a week] initially, and decrease it from there."[59]

---

56. Ibid.

57. Note that this responds to Pitesky, Stackhouse, and Mitloehner's claim that the FAO's report is incomplete because it "does not account for 'default' emissions. Specifically, if domesticated livestock were reduced or even eliminated, the question of what 'substitute' GHGs would be produced in their place has never been estimated." Pitesky, Stackhouse, and Mitloehner, "Clearing the Air," 35. If accurate, Pelletier and Tyedmers's analysis demonstrates that a plant-based diet is likely to be the only sustainable way of feeding the current and projected human population.

58. Pelletier and Tyedmers, "Forecasting," 3.

59. Juliette Jowit, "UN Says Eat Less Meat to Curb Global Warming," *Guardian* (September 6, 2008), *http://bit.ly/1kqPOfn.*

Advocates of meat consumption and livestock production might critique this conclusion, noting that vegetarians and vegans should not presume that the elimination of meat automatically makes their diet environmentally sustainable. The more industrial the agricultural processes involved in producing one's food, whether meat or plants, the greater the ecological impact. Ecologically speaking, a vegetarian diet based on heavily processed meat substitutes made from plants raised in monoculture—a culture dominated by the growth of a single crop—on formerly forested lands using large quantities of pesticides and fertilizers may be *more* ecologically destructive and create more GHG emissions than eating a grass-fed cow.

It is important to recognize that the act of eating (whether plants or animals) is a fundamentally ecological act. The consumption of one organism by another is perhaps the most basic form of ecological relation. The other literally becomes part of one's being. Indeed, *every* organism destroys others so it might live and thrive; such destruction stands at the very heart of the act of living. As the philosopher Alfred North Whitehead noted nearly a century ago: "Life is robbery."[60] Ecologically speaking, the destruction of life composes a vital part of the flow of energy through natural systems. And yet while life does indeed involve robbery, Whitehead recognized that, "the robber requires justification."[61] As moral agents, the robbery of life must be justified.

It would seem, then, that the morality of one's diet is not merely determined by *what* is eaten but also *how* it is produced. Perhaps, the question is not *whether* one's diet is environmentally destructive, but how destructive it is. While there are important, morally relevant differences between plants and animals, vegetarians and vegans should not be seduced into thinking that their hands are clean because they don't eat animals. An appreciation of the embedded nature of human ecological existence makes it clear that no living being has "clean hands." Humans are no exception. It is not possible for humans—or any other living being—to sustain themselves without destroying other life-forms.

---

60. Alfred North Whitehead, *Process and Reality*, corrected ed., ed. Donald Sherburne and David Ray Griffin (New York: Free Press, [1929] 1978), 105.

61. Ibid.

The human population has now passed the 7-billion mark.[62] Over the next forty years (by 2050), the United Nations estimates that at least 2 billion more humans will be born.[63] Those billions of people will need significant quantities of food. If present trends are any indication, much of this food will be in the form of animal products. Is the FAO right that livestock production can be made sustainable through the intensification of livestock production? Or are advocates of the new agrarianism right that the only form of sustainable agriculture is one based on pasture-raised animals? Or in addition to reforming how animals are raised for food, do humans also need to reduce or largely eliminate animals from their diet? On this increasingly small planet, what form of diet is the *most* ethically responsible and environmentally sustainable? And beyond sustainability, what diet might be more in keeping with a view of morality that seeks voluntary simplicity and ecological harmony?

As Lappé argued in her genre-creating book *Diet for a Small Planet*, examining one's diet is a natural way to start the journey toward living more lightly on the land. Eating is among the most fundamental and most intimate acts, as the material people consume becomes part of them. Food practices and habits are deeply ingrained and part of a complex web that includes habit, economics, nutrition, and culture. Yet, as Lappé suggests, although changing what one eats will not change the planet, it can change attitudes and actions, which can in turn change the world.[64] So, should one eat animals on a warming planet? If so, how much, what kind, and why?

For Further Exploration

1. Repeat the footprint activity described in chapter 4 (see activity 3, step 3 under "For Further Exploration") by going to the

---

62. See United States Census Bureau, International Data Base, *www.census.gov/#*.

63. Contrary to its earlier projections, the United Nations is no longer expecting the human population to stabilize midcentury at 9 billion people. According to its most recent estimates, the human population is projected to continue to climb past 10 billion people by 2100.

64. Lappé, *Diet for a Small Planet*, 14.

websites listed and calculating your "ecological footprint" (the amount of land it takes to provide the resources required to sustain a lifestyle). Then use what you learn to consider how your footprint would be affected if you were to reduce your meat consumption by half. What about entirely? How does this affect the number of Earths required if everyone lived like you? Do the results of the exercise affect your assessment of the three scenarios (greater efficiency of meat production, grass-fed and free-range meat production, reduced meat consumption—including vegetarianism and veganism) for addressing the impact of global livestock production? Why or why not?

2. What is the relationship between these three scenarios for reducing the climate impact of livestock and the responses of sustainability, stewardship, and voluntary simplicity (presented in chaps. 4 and 5)?

3. Select an aspect of the typical American's lifestyle (other than the consumption of meat) related to anthropogenic climate change (e.g., air travel, automobile travel, heating of homes) and identify responses advocates of sustainability, stewardship, and voluntary simplicity might recommend to mitigate climate change.

4. Identify the strengths and weaknesses of analyzing aspects of one's lifestyle by considering how advocates of sustainability, stewardship, and voluntary simplicity might respond.

Additional Resources

FOOD AND THE MORAL STATUS OF ANIMALS

Lappé, Francis Moore. *Diet for a Small Planet*. New York: Ballantine Books, [1971] 1991.

Regan, Tom. *The Case for Animal Rights*. Oakland: University of California Press, [1983] 2004.

Singer, Peter. *Animal Liberation*. New York: Harper Perennial, [1975] 2009.

ETHICS AND FOOD

Fairlie, Simon. *Meat: A Benign Extravagance.* White River Junction, VT: Chelsea Green Publishing, 2010.

Foer, Jonathan Safran. *Eating Animals.* New York: Little, Brown, 2009.

Kingsolver, Barbara. *Animal, Vegetable, Miracle.* New York: Harper-Collins, 2007.

Petrini, Carlo. *Slow Food Nation.* New York: Rizzoli Ex Libris, 2007.

Pollan, Michael. *In Defense of Food: An Eater's Manifesto.* New York: Penguin, 2009.

———. *The Omnivore's Dilemma: A Natural History of Four Meals.* New York: Penguin, 2007.

Schlosser, Eric. *Fast Food Nation.* New York: Houghton Mifflin, 2001.

Schlosser, Eric, and Charles Wilson. *Chew on This: Everything You Don't Want to Know about Fast Food.* New York: Houghton Mifflin, 2006.

Singer, Peter, and Jim Mason. *The Ethics of What We Eat: Why Our Food Choices Matter.* New York: Rodale, 2007.

ENVIRONMENTAL IMPACT AND ETHICAL SIGNIFICANCE OF LIVESTOCK PRODUCTION

Foley, Jonathan A. "Can We Feed the World and Sustain the Planet?" *Scientific American* (November 2011): 60–65.

Foley, Jonathan A., et al., "Solutions for a Cultivated Planet." *Nature* 478 (October 20, 2011): 337–42.

Food and Agriculture Organization. *Tackling Climate Change through Livestock: A Global Assessment of Emissions and Mitigation Opportunities.* Rome: Food and Agriculture Organization, 2013.

Henning, Brian G. "Standing in Livestock's 'Long Shadow': The Ethics of Eating Meat on a Small Planet." *Ethics & the Environment* 16, no. 2 (2011): 63–94.

Pelletier, Nathan, and Peter Tyedmers. "Forecasting Potential Global Environmental Costs of Livestock Production 2000–2050."

Proceedings of the National Academy of Science 107, no. 43 (October 26, 2010).

Stănescu, Vasile. "'Green' Eggs and Ham? The Myth of Sustainable Meat and the Danger of the Local." *Journal for Critical Animal Studies* 8 (2010).

Steinfeld, Henning, and Pierre Gerber. "Livestock Production and the Global Environment: Consume Less or Produce Better?" *Proceedings of the National Academy of Science* 107, no. 43 (October 26, 2010), 18237–38.

Steinfeld, Henning, Pierre Gerber, Tom Wassenaar, Vincent Castel, Mauricio Rosales, and Cees de Haan. *Livestock's Long Shadow: Environmental Issues and Options.* Rome: Food and Agriculture Organization, 2006.

Thompson, Paul B. "The Agricultural Ethics of Biofuels: The Food vs. Fuel Debate." *Agriculture* 2 (2012): 339–58.

VIDEOS ON THE ETHICS OF EATING

Fulkerson, Lee. *Forks Over Knives* Directed by Lee Fulkerson. Monica Beach Media, 2011, 90 minutes.

Kenner, Robert, Elise Pearlstein, and Kim Roberts. *Food, Inc.* Directed by Robert Kenner. New York: Magnolia Pictures, 2008, 94 minutes.

Schlosser, Eric, and Richard Linklater. *Fast Food Nation.* Directed by Richard Linklater. Hollywood, CA: 20th Century Fox, 2006, 116 minutes.

The True Cost of Food. San Francisco: Sierra Club, 2005, 15 minutes. Available online on the Sierra Club's website, *http://bit .ly/1octEyx*.

Glossary

acidification Ocean acidification is the on-going decrease in the pH of Earth's oceans caused by the absorption of carbon dioxide (CO_2) from the atmosphere.

ad hominem Logicians refer to an assault on the character of the agent—as opposed to a critique of the veracity of the argument or statement—as an *ad hominem* attack.

albedo From the Latin *albus* ("white"), albedo refers to the fraction of solar energy (shortwave or ultraviolet radiation) reflected from Earth back into space (longwave or infrared radiation). It is a measure of the reflectivity of Earth's surface. Dark surfaces have a lower albedo (are less reflective) than light colored surfaces.

anthropocentric All and only human beings have intrinsic value. All other beings are only valuable insofar as they are valued by human beings, but have no value in their own right.

anthropogenic From the ancient Greek *anthropos* ("human") and *genesis* ("cause"), this refers to changes brought about by human activity.

axiology That branch of philosophy that studies different theories as to the nature and extent of value.

carbon neutrality Defined as having zero net GHG emissions. This is achieved by reducing GHG emissions as much as possible and then using carbon offsets to mitigate the remaining emissions.

category error A type of informal logical fallacy committed when things of one sort are presented as if they belonged to another. For instance, the claim "taxes are low in fat" is a category error. The problem is that taxes (one type of thing) are not the sort of thing that are eaten (another category of thing) and that can be low in fat.

climate The prevailing weather conditions of a region averaged over a long period of time. Climate change thus refers to changes in long-term averages of daily weather.

Conference of the Parties (COP) The main body of the UNFCC. A primary task of the COP is to review the emission inventories submitted by all the states that are parties to the UNFCCC or Convention. The COP usually meets once a year to review progress. In this context, "conference" means "association" more than "meeting."

consensus From the Latin *consensus*, meaning "agreement"; this refers to agreement in opinion among a number of persons.

consilience Coined by the biologist William Whewell in 1840, this refers literally to the "jumping together" or concurrence of many different facts.

direct moral duty A moral duty owed to another being for its own sake because it has intrinsic value. For instance, I ought not to kick my brother for his sake, because he has intrinsic value.

dystopia The inverse of a utopia or the worst possible world.

evidence Facts taken together that either confirm or disconfirm a hypothesis or theory.

externalities Costs associated with a product or activity that are not reflected in the price paid by the consumer. A result of externalities is that the (private) costs of production tend to be lower than the actual (social) costs.

facts Particular observations that may or may not support a hypothesis or theory.

false dichotomy or false dilemma An informal logical fallacy committed when one is forced to choose among an artificially short and usually exaggerated list of choices when more options are available.

false equivalence A real or perceived bias in which an issue is presented as being more balanced between opposing viewpoints than the evidence actually supports.

greenhouse effect The molecules in Earth's atmosphere transmit shortwave solar radiation but trap longwave solar radiation, much like a greenhouse, making the temperature on Earth's surface much warmer than the temperature outside Earth's atmosphere.

indirect moral duty A moral duty owed to another being, not for its own sake, but for the sake of another being, to which direct duties are owed. For instance, I ought not to kick your car tires, not because I owe anything to your car (direct duty), but because I owe it to you as the car's owner (indirect duty).

inductive Characteristic of an argument that is more or less probable, given the strength of the premises that are based on particular observations over a given time.

instrumental value The value of a being due to its usefulness.

intrinsic value The value of a being for its own sake, separate from its usefulness.

Milankovitch cycles Periodic variations in Earth's position relative to the Sun as Earth orbits, affecting the distribution of solar radiation.

moral duty, direct A moral duty owed to another being for its own sake because it has intrinsic value. For instance, I ought not to kick my brother for his sake, because he has intrinsic value.

moral duty, indirect A moral duty owed to another being, not for its own sake, but for the sake of another being, to which direct duties are owed. For instance, I ought not to kick your car tires, not because I owe anything to your car (direct duty), but because I owe it to you as the car's owner (indirect duty).

natural variability Refers to the regular variability of Earth's weather and climate. Weather in particular regions varies, with some periods hotter than normal and some periods colder than normal. Climate also varies, with Earth regularly undergoing glacial and interglacial periods of change over thousands of years.

peer review The evaluation of the work of another by one or more experts (without conflict of interest) in the relevant field in order to ensure the quality, accuracy, and value of the work.

positive feedback Feedback in which a system responds to a perturbation in the same direction as the perturbation. One example of positive feedback in the climate is the melting of the Arctic ice cap. Higher concentrations of CO_2 causes an increase in temperature (perturbation), which causes sea ice to retreat, leaving more open ocean. The open ocean has a lower albedo, reflecting less incoming radiation, which causes an increase in temperature (the same direction as the perturbation).

salinization In the context of climate change, this refers to the encroachment of salt water into freshwater estuaries and aquifers due to rising sea levels.

scientific law A scientific theory accepted as a valid explanation of a phenomenon usually after being inductively supported and tested over a long period of time.

scientific theory A scientific hypothesis that is inductively supported and tested over a long period of time.

scope of direct moral consideration Those beings deserving moral consideration (owed direct duties) for their own sake because of their intrinsic value.

standard of living An individual's or household's level of wealth and comfort, as measured by income and consumption of goods and services.

subsidy Money granted by a government to an individual or company to assist an enterprise.

technophilia The love of technology, from the ancient Greek *techne* (from which the modern word *technology* is derived) and *philia* ("love").

theocentrism The belief that a divine being is the sole source of all meaning and value. All other beings are only valuable insofar as they are related to the divine being.

United Nations Framework Convention on Climate Change (UNFCCC) The 1992 international treaty (often referred to as the Convention) created by the international community to limit average global temperature increases and to help states adapt to climate change impacts. The treaty was ratified by 166 countries and came into legal force on March 21, 1994.

weather The current conditions of the atmosphere, including wind, temperature, precipitation, pressure, and cloud cover.

Bibliography

Aiken, Scott F. "The Significance of Al Gore's Purported Hypocrisy." *Environmental Ethics* 31 (2009): 111–12.

Aiken, Scott F., and Robert B. Tallisse. "The Truth about Hypocrisy: Charges of Hypocrisy Can Be Surprisingly Irrelevant and Often Distract Us from More Important Concerns." *Scientific American*, December 3, 2008.

Alexander, Samuel, et al. *Voluntary Simplicity: The Poetic Alternative to Consumer Culture.* New Zealand: Stead & Daughters, 2009.

American College & University Presidents' Climate Commitment. Last modified 2014. Accessed November 28, 2014. *http://www.presidentsclimatecommitment.org.*

———. "The ACUPCC Voluntary Carbon Offset Protocol." Accessed November 28, 2014. *http://bit.ly/1kcoGvC.*

———. "Text of the American College & University Presidents' Climate Commitment." Last modified 2013. *http://bit.ly/1lPmhs2.*

———. "ACUPCC Progress Summary." June 2013. *http://bit.ly/TR7aZ3.*

American Dietetic Association. "Position of the American Dietetic Association: Vegetarian Diets." *Journal of the American Dietetic Association* 109, no. 7 (2009), 1266–978.

American Lung Association. "Toxic Air: Time to Clean Up Coal-fired Power Plants." March 8, 2011. *http://www.lung.org/about-us/our-impact/top-stories/toxic-air-coal-fired-power-plants.html.*

Architecture 2030. "Hot Topics: Nation Under Siege." Accessed November 28, 2014. *http://architecture2030.org/hot_topics/nation_under_siege.*

Association for the Advancement of Sustainability in Higher Education. Accessed November 28, 2014. *http://www.aashe.org.*

Attfield, Robin. "Beyond the Earth Charter: Taking Possible People Seriously." *Environmental Ethics* 29 (2007): 359–67.

———. *Environmental Ethics.* Oxford: Polity, 2003.

————. *The Ethics of the Global Environment*. West Lafayette, IN: Purdue University Press, 1999.

Baroni, L., L. Cenci, M. Tettamanti, and M. Berati. "Evaluating the Environmental Impact of Various Dietary Patterns Combined with Different Forms of Production Systems." *European Journal of Clinical Nutrition* 61 (2007): 279–86.

Barry, Brian. "Sustainability and Intergenerational Justice." In *Environmental Ethics: An Anthology*, edited by Holmes Rolston III and Andrew Light, 487–99. Oxford: Blackwell, 2003.

Berry, Thomas. *The Great Work: Our Way into the Future*. New York: Three Rivers Press, 1999.

Berry, Wendell. "Christianity and the Survival of Creation." *Cross Currents* 43, no. 2 (Summer 1993). *http://www.crosscurrents.org/berry.htm*.

Birge, Mary Katherine. "Genesis." In *Genesis, Evolution, and the Search for a Reasoned Faith*, edited by Mary Katherine Birge, Brian G. Henning, Rodica M. M. Stoicoiu, and Ryan Taylor, 1–40. Winona, MN: Anselm Academic, 2011.

Broder, John M. "E.P.A. Will Delay Rule Limiting Carbon Emissions at New Power Plants." *New York Times*, April 12, 2013. *http://nyti.ms/TR3Vkf*.

Broome, John. "A Philosopher at the IPCC." International Society for Environmental Ethics (website), May 20, 2014. *http://bit.ly/RxDr59*.

Carbon Dioxide Information Analysis Center. "Recent Greenhouse Gas Concentrations." Accessed November 28, 2014. *http://cdiac.ornl.gov/pns/current_ghg.html*.

Cafaro, Philip. "Economic Growth or the Flourishing Life: The Ethical Choice Climate Change Puts to Humanity." *Essays in Philosophy* 11, no. 1 (2010): 44-75.

————. "Taming Growth and Articulating a Sustainable Future: The Way Forward for Environmental Ethics." *Ethics & the Environment* 16, no. 1 (2011): 1–23.

Callicott, J. Baird. *In Defense of the Land Ethic: Essays in Environmental Philosophy*. Albany: State University of New York Press, 1989.

————. *Thinking Like a Planet: The Land Ethic and the Earth Ethic*. New York: Oxford University Press, 2014.

Christiansen, Drew, and Walter Grazer, eds. *"And God Saw That It Was Good": Catholic Theology and the Environment*. Washington, DC: United States Catholic Conference, 1996.

Clifford, Anne M. "Foundations for a Catholic Ecological Theology of God." In *"And God Saw That It Was Good": Catholic Theology and the Environment*, edited by Drew Christiansen and Walter Grazer, 19–46. Washington DC: United States Catholic Conference, 1996.

Climate Central. "Surging Seas." Accessed November 28, 2014. *http:// sealevel.climatecentral.org/*.

CO2 Now. Accessed November 28, 2014. *http://co2now.org/*.

The Consensus Project. Accessed November 28, 2014. *http://theconsensus project.com/*.

Cook, John, et al. "Quantifying the Consensus on Anthropogenic Global Warming in the Scientific Literature." *Environmental Research Letters*, January 18, 2013. doi:10.1088/1748-9326/8/2/024024.Dalai Lama. *Ethics for the New Millennium*. New York: Riverhead, 1999.

Daly, Herman. *Ecological Economics and Sustainable Development: Selected Essays of Herman Daly*. Cheltenham, UK: Edward Elgar, 2007.

de Graaf, John, David Wann, and Thomas H. Naylor. *Affluenza: The All-Consuming Epidemic*. 2nd ed. San Francisco: Berrett-Koehler, 2005.

Devall, Bill, and George Sessions. *Deep Ecology: Living as If Nature Mattered*. Salt Lake City, UT: Gibbs Smith, 1985.

Doran, Peter T., and Maggie Kendall Zimmerman. "Examining the Scientific Consensus on Climate Change." *Eos* 90, no. 3 (January 2009): 22.

Earth Day Network. "Footprint Calculator." Accessed November 28, 2014. *http://bit.ly/1Jf68Rg*.

Ecological Footprint. Accessed November 28, 2014. *http://www.ecological footprint.org/*.

Elgin, Duane. *Voluntary Simplicity: Toward a Way of Life That Is Outwardly Simple, Inwardly Rich*. 2nd ed. New York: Harper, 2010.

Environmental Protection Agency. "Frequently Asked Questions about Global Warming and Global Climate Change: Back to Basics." Accessed November 28, 2014. *http://www.epa.gov/climatechange /Downloads/ghgemissions/Climate_Basics.pdf*.

———. "Household Carbon Footprint Calculator." Accessed November 28, 2014. *http://1.usa.gov/1dKe1ao*.

———. "Individual Greenhouse Gas Emissions Calculator." Accessed November 28, 2014. *http://1.usa.gov/1kcpdh7*.

Fairlie, Simon. *Meat: A Benign Extravagance.* White River Junction, VT: Chelsea Green, 2010.

Fiala, Nathan. "Meeting the Demand: An Estimation of Potential Future Greenhouse Gas Emissions from Meat Production." *Ecological Economics* 67 (2008): 412–19.

FitzPatrick, William J. "Climate Change and the Rights of Future Generations: Social Justice Beyond Mutual Advantage." *Environmental Ethics* 29 (2007): 369–88

Flannery, Tim. *The Weather Makers: How Man Is Changing the Climate and What It Means for Life on Earth.* New York: Atlantic Monthly Press, 2005.

Foer, Jonathan Safran. *Eating Animals.* New York: Little, Brown, 2009.

Foley, Jonathan A. "Can We Feed the World and Sustain the Planet?" *Scientific American,* November 2011, 60–65.

Foley, Jonathan A., et al. "Solutions for a Cultivated Planet." *Nature* 478 (October 20, 2011): 337–42.

Food and Agriculture Organization. *Tackling Climate Change through Livestock: A Global Assessment of Emissions and Mitigation Opportunities.* Rome: Food and Agriculture Organization, 2013.

Fouts, Roger, and Stephen Tukel Mills. *Next of Kin: My Conversations with Chimpanzees.* New York: Avon Books, 1997.

Fulkerson, Lee. *Forks Over Knives.* Directed by Lee Fulkerson. Monica Beach Media, 2011, 90 minutes.

Gabbard, Alex. "Coal Combustion: Nuclear Resource or Danger." Last modified February 5, 2008. *http://1.usa.gov/1jY7Q8e.*

Gardiner, Stephen M. "Ethics and Global Climate Change." *Ethics* 114 (April 2004): 555–600.

———. "A Perfect Moral Storm: Climate Change, Intergenerational Ethics, and the Problem of Corruption." *Environmental Values* 15 (2006): 397–413.

———. *A Perfect Moral Storm: The Ethical Tragedy of Climate Change.* Oxford: Oxford University Press, 2011.

———. "The Pure Intergenerational Problem." *The Monist* 86, no. 3 (2003): 481–500.

Gardiner, Stephen M., Simon Caney, Dale Jamieson, and Henry Shue, eds. *Climate Ethics: Essential Readings.* New York: Oxford, 2010.

Gillis, Justin, and Kenneth Chang. "Scientists Warn of Rising Oceans from Polar Melt." *New York Times*, May 12, 2014. *http://nyti.ms/1iGkKCF.*

Global Warming Petition Project. Accessed November 28, 2014. *http://www.petitionproject.org/.*

Golding, Martin. "Limited Obligations to Future Generations." *The Monist* 56 (1972): 85–99.

Gould, Stephen J. "The Golden Rule: A Proper Scale for Our Environmental Crisis." *Natural History* 99, no. 9 (September 1990): 24. Halweil, Brian. "Meat Production Continues to Rise." *Worldwatch Institute*, August 20, 2008, p. 2, *http://www.worldwatch.org/node/5443/.*

Hansen, James E. "Climate Change Is Here—And Worse than We Thought." *Washington Post*, August 3, 2012. *http://wapo.st/1kHRrF6.*

Hardin, Garrett. "Who Cares for Posterity?" In *The Limits of Altruism*. Indianapolis: Indiana University Press, 1977.

Hargrove, Eugene. "The Historical Foundations of American Environmental Attitudes." *Environmental Ethics* 1 (1979): 209–40.

Heilbroner, Robert. "What Has Posterity Ever Done for Me?" *New York Times Magazine*, January 19, 1975.

Henning, Brian G. *The Ethics of Creativity: Beauty, Morality, and Nature in a Processive Cosmos*. Pittsburgh: University of Pittsburgh Press, 2005.

———. "From Despot to Steward: The Greening of Catholic Social Teaching." In *The Heart of Catholic Social Teaching: Its Origins and Contemporary Significance*, edited by David Matzko McCarthy, 83–194. Grand Rapids, MI: Brazos, 2009.

———. "From Exception to Exemplification: Understanding the Debate over Darwin." In *Genesis, Evolution, and the Search for a Reasoned Faith*, edited by Mary Katherine Birge, Brian G. Henning, Rodica M. M. Stoicoiu, and Ryan Taylor, 73–98. Winona, MN: Anselm Academic, 2011.

———. "Standing in Livestock's 'Long Shadow': The Ethics of Eating Meat on a Small Planet." *Ethics & the Environment* 16, no. 2 (2011): 63–94.

———. "Sustainability and Other Ecological Mistakes." In *Beyond Superlatives*, edited by Roland Faber, J. R. Hustwit, and Hollis Phelps, 76–89. Newcastle upon Tyne: Cambridge Scholars Press, 2014.

———. "Trusting in the 'Efficacy of Beauty': A Kalocentric Approach to Moral Philosophy." *Ethics & the Environment* 14, no. 1 (2009): 101–28.

Houghton, John. *Global Warming: The Complete Briefing.* 4th ed. Cambridge: Cambridge University Press, 2009.

Intergovernmental Panel on Climate Change. *Climate Change 2014: Mitigation of Climate Change.* 2014. *http://mitigation2014.org/report/.*

———. "Fifth Assessment Report: Working Group I, Summary for Policymakers." *Climate Change 2013: The Physical Basis,* September 27, 2013. *http://www.climatechange2013.org/spm.*

———. "First Assessment Report: Working Group I, Policymakers Summary." 1990. *http://bit.ly/1tLUE9C.*

———. "Fourth Assessment Report: Frequently Asked Questions." Accessed November 29, 2014. *www.ipcc.ch/publications_and_data /ar4/wg1/en/faq-6-1.html.*

———. *Fourth Assessment Report.* Working Group I, 2007. *http://bit .ly/1wppjKS.*

———. "History." Accessed November 29, 2014. *http://bit.ly/1nxrB7L.*

Izzi Deen, Mawil Y. "Islamic Environmental Ethics, Law, and Society." In *Environmental Ethics: Divergence & Convergence,* 3rd ed., edited by Susan J. Armstrong and Richard G. Botzler. New York: McGrawHill, 2004.

Jamieson, Dale. "Ethics, Public Policy, and Global Warming." *Science, Technology, & Human Values* 17 (April 1992): 139–53.

———. *Reason in a Dark Time: Why the Struggle against Climate Change Failed—And What It Means for Our Future.* Oxford: Oxford University Press, 2014.

Jowit, Juliette. "UN Says Eat Less Meat to Curb Global Warming." *Guardian,* September 6, 2008. *http://bit.ly/1kqPOfn.*

Kant, Immanuel. *Grounding for the Metaphysics of Morals.* Translated by James W. Ellington. Indianapolis, IN: Hackett, 1981.

———. *Lectures on Ethics.* Translated by Louis Infield. London: Methuen, 1930.

Kenner, Robert, Elise Pearlstein, and Kim Roberts. *Food, Inc.* Directed by Robert Kenner. New York: Magnolia Pictures, 2008, 94 minutes.

King, Martin Luther, Jr. "I Have a Dream (Lincoln Memorial, Washington, DC, August 28, 1963)." In *I Have a Dream: Writings and Speeches that Changed the World*, edited by James M. Washington. San Francisco: Harper SanFrancisco, 1992.

———. "The Quest for Peace and Justice." December 11, 1964, Nobelprize. org. *http://bit.ly/1hTXCWf.*

———. "Letter from a Birmingham Jail (1963)." In *I Have a Dream: Writings and Speeches that Changed the World*, edited by James M. Washington. San Francisco: HarperSanFrancisco, 1992.

———. "Whitehead, Alfred North." *The King Center* (website). Accessed November 29, 2014. *www.thekingcenter.org/archive/theme/4465.*

Kingsolver, Barbara. *Animal, Vegetable, Miracle.* New York: HarperCollins, 2007.

Kolbert, Elizabeth. *The Sixth Extinction: An Unnatural History.* New York: Henry Holt, 2014.

Lachs, John. "Good Enough." *Journal of Speculative Philosophy* 23, no. 1 (2009): 1–7.

Lappé, Francis Moore. *Diet for a Small Planet.* New York: Ballantine Books, [1971] 1991.

Leopold, Aldo. *A Sand County Almanac and Sketches Here and There.* New York: Oxford University Press, [1949] 1987.

"Light, Andrew." George Mason University, Institute for Philosophy and Public Policy, Accessed November 29, 2014. *http://ippp.gmu.edu/people/light.html.*

Light, Andrew. "The Bridge to the Durban Outcome" (image). In "Why Durban Matters: International Climate Process Strengthened at South Africa Talks." Center for American Progress (website), December 19, 2011. *http://bit.ly/1ioKCUx.*

———. "Why Durban Matters: International Climate Process Strengthened at South Africa Talks." Center for American Progress (website), December 19, 2011. *http://bit.ly/1ioKCUx.*

Light, Andrew, Rebecca Lefton, Adam James, Gwynne Taraska, and Katie Valentine. "Doha Climate Summit Ends with the Long March to 2015." Center for American Progress (website), December 11, 2012. *http://bit.ly/1mlVoO5.*

Locke, John. *Second Treatise of Government.* Edited by C. B. Macpherson. Indianapolis, IN: Hackett, 1980.

Lovelock, James. *The Vanishing Face of Gaia: A Final Warning.* New York: Basic Books, 2009.

McKibben, Bill. *Eaarth: Making a Life on a Tough New Planet.* New York: Time Books, 2010.

————. *Deep Economy: The Wealth of Communities and the Durable Future.* New York: Times Books, 2010.

————. "Global Warming's Terrifying New Math." *Rolling Stone,* July 19, 2012. *http://rol.st/1bYUwIk.*

————. *Oil and Honey: The Education of an Unlikely Activist.* New York: Times Books, 2013.

McMichael, Anthony J., J. W. Powles, C. D. Butler, and R. Uauy. "Energy and Health 5: Food, Livestock Production, Energy, Climate Change, and Health." *The Lancet* 370 (2007): 1253–63.

Milbrath, Lester. "Redefining the Good Life in a Sustainable Society." *Environmental Values* 2, no. 3 (August 1993): 261–69.

Mill, John Stuart. *Utilitarianism, On Liberty, and Essay on Bentham: Together with Selected Writings of Jeremy Bentham and John Austin.* Edited by Mary Warnock. New York: Meridian Books, 1962.

Miller, R. L. "Attack of the Climate Zombies!" *Climate Progress* (blog), September 10, 2010. *http://bit.ly/1kkKlXA.*

MIT Joint Program on the Science and Policy of Global Change Greenhouse Gamble Wheels. Accessed November 29, 2014. *http://global change.mit.edu/focus-areas/uncertainty/gamble.*

Moncrief, Lewis W. "The Cultural Basis for Our Environmental Crisis: Judeo-Christian Tradition Is Only One of Many Cultural Factors Contributing to the Environmental Crisis." *Science* 170 (1970): 508–12.

Muskal, Michael. "As Drought Widens, 50.3% of U.S. Counties Declared Disaster Areas." *Los Angeles Times,* August 1, 2012. *http://lat .ms/1yOTbPL.*

Nash, James A. *Loving Nature: Ecological Integrity and Christian Responsibility.* Nashville, TN: Abingdon, 1991.

National Center for Atmospheric Research. "Record High Temperatures Far Outpace Record Lows across U.S." *AtmosNews,* November 12, 2009. *http://bit.ly/1pfvP5Y.*

National Geographic. "Rising Seas." Accessed November 29, 2014. *http://ngm.nationalgeographic.com/2013/09/rising-seas/if -ice-melted-map.*

National Oceanic and Atmospheric Administration. "Human and Economic Indicators—Shishmaref." Accessed November 29, 2014. *http://www .arctic.noaa.gov/detect/human-shishmaref.shtml.*

————. National Climatic Data Center. Accessed November 29, 2014. *http://www.ncdc.noaa.gov.*

———. "State of the Climate." Accessed November 29, 2014. *http:/www .ncdc.noaa.gov/sotc/*.

———. "State of the Climate: Global Analysis for July 2012." Accessed November 29, 2014. *http://www.ncdc.noaa.gov/sotc/global/2012/7*.

———. "State of the Climate: National Overview for June 2012." Accessed November 29, 2014. *http://www.ncdc.noaa.gov/sotc/national/2012/6*.

National Snow & Ice Data Center (2012). "A Most Interesting Arctic Summer." Accessed November 29, 2014. *http://nsidc.org/arcticsea icenews/2012/08/a-most-interesting-arctic-summer/*.

National Speech and Debate Association. "Past Policy Topics." Accessed November 29, 2014. *http://www.speechanddebate.org/pastpolicytopics*.

The Nature Conservancy. "What's My Carbon Footprint?" Accessed November 29, 2014. *http://bit.ly/1cXA1QX*.

Nordhaus, William, David Popp, Zili Yang, Joseph Boyer et al. RICE and DICE Models of Economics of Climate Change. Accessed November 29, 2014. *http://www.econ.yale.edu/~nordhaus/homepage/dicemodels.htm*.

Norton, Bryan G. "Integration or Reduction: Two Approaches to Environmental Values." In *Environmental Pragmatism*, edited by Andrew Light and Eric Katz, 105–38. New York: Routledge, 1996.

———. *Searching for Sustainability: Interdisciplinary Essays in the Philosophy of Conservation Biology*. Cambridge: Cambridge University Press, 2003.

Oldham, Jennifer, Amanda J. Crawford, and Tim Jones. "Colorado Wildfire Forces 34,500 to Evacute as Homes Burn." *BloombergBusinessweek*, June 28, 2014. *http://buswk.co/1vhyFrR*.

Organisation for Economic Co-operation and Development. *Climate and Carbon: Aligning Prices and Policies*. October 9, 2013. *http://www .oecd.org/greengrowth/climate-carbon.htm*.

———. *OECD Environmental Outlook to 2030: Executive Summary*. 2008, p. 7. *http://bit.ly/Scpx9r*.

Oreskes, Naomi. "The Scientific Consensus on Climate Change: How Do We Know We're Not Wrong?" In *Climate Change: What It Means for Us, Our Children, and Our Grandchildren*, edited by Joseph F. C. DiMento and Pamela Doughman, 65–100. Cambridge, MA: MIT Press, 2007.

Oreskes, Naomi, and Erik M. Conway. *Merchants of Doubt: How a Handful of Scientists Obscured the Truth on Issues from Tobacco Smoke to Global Warming*. New York: Bloomsbury, 2010.

Orr, David. *Earth in Mind: On Education, Environment, and the Human Prospect.* Washington, DC: Island Press, 2004.

———. *Ecological Literacy: Education and the Transition to a Postmodern World.* Albany: State University of New York Press, 1992.

———. "Four Challenges of Sustainability." *Conservation Biology* 16, no. 6 (December 2002): 1457–60.

Palmer, Clare. "Stewardship: A Case Study in Environmental Ethics." In *The Earth Beneath*, edited by Ian Ball, Margaret Goodall, Clare Palmer, and John Reader, 67–86. London: SPCK, 1992.

Parfit, Derek. "Energy Policy and the Further Future: The Identity Problem." In *Climate Ethics: Essential Readings*, edited by Stephen M. Gardiner, Simon Caney, Dale Jamieson, and Henry Shue, 112–21. New York: Oxford University Press, 2010.

Pelletier, Nathan, and Peter Tyedmers. "Forecasting Potential Global Environmental Costs of Livestock Production 2000–2050. *Proceedings of the National Academy of Science* 107, no. 43 (October 26, 2010): 1–4.

Petrini, Carlo. *Slow Food Nation.* New York: Rizzoli Ex Libris, 2007.

Pew Research Center. "Climate Change: Key Data Points from Pew Research." January 27, 2014. *http://bit.ly/1f9FUJe.*

———. "Fewer Americans See Solid Evidence of Global Warming." October 22, 2009. *http://bit.ly/1nQJZXx.*

Pitesky, Maurice E., Kimberly R. Stackhouse, and Frank M. Mitloehner. "Clearing the Air: Livestock's Contribution to Climate Change." In *Advances in Agronomy*, vol. 103, edited by Donald Sparks, 1–40. Burlington, MA: Academic Press, 2009.

Pollan, Michael. *In Defense of Food: An Eater's Manifesto.* New York: Penguin, 2009.

———. *The Omnivore's Dilemma: A Natural History of Four Meals.* New York: Penguin, 2007.

Pope John Paul II. "Peace with God the Creator, Peace with All of Creation." January 1, 1990. *http://bit.ly/1nsMbbQ.*

Regan, Tom. *The Case for Animal Rights.* Oakland, CA: University of California Press, [1983] 2004.

———. "Work, Hypocrisy, and Integrity." In *Defending Animal Rights*, 164–75. Urbana: University of Illinois Press, 2001.

Richardson, Katherine, et al. "Synthesis Report." In *Climate Change: Global Risks, Challenges & Decisions*, International Scientific Congress, Copenhagen, March 10–12, 2009, p. 14. *http://bit.ly/1wwamru.*

Rock Ethics Institute. Accessed November 29, 2014. *http://rockethics.psu .edu/*.

———. "Ethics in Climate Change." Accessed November 29, 2014. *http:// rockethics.psu.edu/climate/*.

———. "Ethical Dimensions of Climate Change." Accessed November 29, 2014. *http://rockethics.psu.edu/climate/edcc*.

———. "The Gender Justice and Global Climate Change Network." Accessed November 29, 2014. *http://rockethics.psu.edu/climate/g2c2*.

———. "Sustainability Ethics." Accessed November 29, 2014. *http://rock ethics.psu.edu/climate/sustainability-ethics*.

Rockström, Johan, et al. "A Safe Operating Space for Humanity." *Nature* 461, no. 7263 (September 24, 2009): 472–75.

Rolston, Holmes, III. *Environmental Ethics: Duties to and Values in the Natural World*. Philadelphia: Temple University Press, 1988.

Ruth, Matthias, Dana Coelho, and Daria Karetnikov. *The US Economic Impacts of Climate Change and the Costs of Inaction*. College Park: University of Maryland, 2007. *http://bit.ly/ScplH7*.

Schlosser, Eric. *Fast Food Nation*. New York: Houghton Mifflin, 2001.

Schlosser, Eric, and Richard Linklater. *Fast Food Nation*. Directed by Richard Linklater. Hollywood, CA: 20th Century Fox, 2006, 116 minutes.

Schlosser, Eric, and Charles Wilson. *Chew on This: Everything You Don't Want to Know About Fast Food*. New York: Houghton Mifflin, 2006.

Shellenberger, Michael, and Ted Nordhaus. "The Death of Environmentalism: Global Warming Politics in a Post-Environmental World." The Breakthrough Institute (website), June 16, 2010. *http://bit.ly/ScPdTf*.

Sherman, Daniel J. "Sustainability: What's the Big Idea? A Strategy for Transforming the Higher Education Curriculum." *Sustainability* 1, no. 3 (2008): 188–95.

Shue, Henry. "Global Environment and International Inequity." In *Climate Ethics: Essential Readings*, edited by Stephen M. Gardiner, Simon Caney, Dale Jamieson, and Henry Shue, 101–11. Oxford: Oxford University Press, 2010.

Simple Living Institute. Accessed November 29, 2014. *http://www.simple-livinginstitute.org*.

Simplicity Institute. Accessed November 29, 2014. *http://simplicityinstitute.org/*.

Singer, Peter. *Animal Liberation*. Updated ed. New York: Harper Perennial, [1975] 2009.

———. "One Atmosphere." In *One World: The Ethics of Globalization*, 14–50. New Haven, CT: Yale University Press, 2002.

Singer, Peter, and Jim Mason. *The Ethics of What We Eat: Why Our Food Choices Matter*. New York: Rodale, 2007.

Skeptical Science. Accessed November 29, 2014. *http://www.skeptical science.com*.

Slivka, Kelly. "Record High Temperatures in First Six Months of the Year." *New York Times*, July 9, 2012. *http://nyti.ms/TQE7ox*.

Stănescu, Vasile. "'Green' Eggs and Ham? The Myth of Sustainable Meat and the Danger of the Local." *Journal for Critical Animal Studies* 8 (2010): 8–32.

Steinfeld, Henning, and Pierre Gerber. "Livestock Production and the Global Environment: Consume Less or Produce Better?" *Proceedings of the National Academy of Science* 107, no. 43 (October 26, 2010): 18237–38.

Steinfeld, Henning, Pierre Gerber, Tom Wassenaar, Vincent Castel, Mauricio Rosales, and Cees de Haan. *Livestock's Long Shadow: Environmental Issues and Options*. Rome: Food and Agriculture Organization, 2006.

Stern, Nicholas. *The Economics of Climate Change: The Stern Review*. Cambridge: Cambridge University Press, 2007.

Stone, Michael K., and Zenobia Barlow, eds. *Ecological Literacy: Educating Our Children for a Sustainable World*. San Francisco: Sierra Club Books, 2005.

The Story of Stuff Project. Accessed November 29, 2014. *http://storyof stuff.org/*.

Sun Come Up. Directed by Jennifer Redfearn. Blooming Grove, NY: New Day Films, 2010, 39 minutes. *http://www.suncomeup.com/*.

Sustainability Research Institute. Accessed November 29, 2014. *http:// www.see.leeds.ac.uk/research/sri/*.Thompson, Paul B. "The Agricultural Ethics of Biofuels: The Food vs. Fuel Debate." *Agriculture* 2 (2012): 339–58. doi:10.3390/agriculture2040339.

Timmons, Mark. "Introduction to Moral Theory: The Nature and Evaluation of Moral Theories." In *Conduct and Character: Readings in Moral Theory*, 6th ed., 1–16. Boston: Wadsworth, 2012.

Troster, Lawrence. "Created in the Image of God: Humanity and Divinity in an Age of Environmentalism." In *Environmental Ethics: Divergence*

& *Convergence*, 3rd ed., edited by Susan J. Armstrong and Richard G. Botzler. New York: McGrawHill, 2004.

The True Cost of Food. San Francisco: Sierra Club, 2005, 15 minutes. *http://bit.ly/1octEyx*.

United Nations Environment Programme. *Rio Declaration on Environment and Development*. Accessed November 29, 2014. *http://bit .ly/1jqNrnN*.

United Nations Framework Convention on Climate Change. "UNFCCC: 20 Years of Effort and Achievement." Accessed November 29, 2014. *http://unfccc.int/timeline*.

United Nations General Assembly. *Report of the World Commission on Environment and Development*. A/RES/42/187, 96th Plenary Meeting, December 11, 1987. *http://www.un-documents.net/wced-ocf.htm*.

United States Census Bureau. Accessed November 29, 2014. *http://www .census.gov/*.

United States Global Change Research Program. Accessed November 29, 2014. *http://ncadac.globalchange.gov/*.

Varner, Gary. "Biocentric Individualism." In *Environmental Ethics: Divergence and Convergence*. 3rd ed., edited by Susan J. Armstrong and Richard G. Botzler, 356–67. New York: McGrawHill, 2004.

White, Lynn, Jr. "The Historical Roots of Our Ecologic Crisis." *Science* 155 (March 10, 1967): 1203–7.

Whitehead, Alfred North. *Adventures of Ideas*. New York: Macmillan, 1933.

———. *The Function of Reason*. Princeton: Princeton University Press, 1929.

———. *Process and Reality*. Corrected ed., edited by Donald Sherburne and David Ray Griffin. New York: Free Press, [1929] 1978.

Whitney, Elspeth. "Lynn White, Ecotheology, and History." *Environmental Ethics* 15 (Summer 1993): 151–69.

World Bank for 2010. "CO2 Emissions." Accessed November 29, 2014. *http://bit.ly/1h4shNk*.

Yale Project on Climate Change Communication. "What's in a Name? Global Warming vs. Climate Change." May 2014. *http://bit.ly/1wfarzH*.

Index

The abbreviations *c, i, s, t,* or *n* that follow page numbers indicate charts, illustrations, sidebars, tables, or footnotes, respectively.